SOUL SIGNS

fire *earth* *air* *water* *sulphur*

SOUL SIGNS

AN ELEMENTAL GUIDE
TO YOUR
SPIRITUAL DESTINY

ROSEMARY ALTEA

RODALE

First published 2004
First published in paperback 2005

Printed in the United States of America
Rodale Inc. makes every effort to use acid-free ⊗, recycled paper ♻.

Book design and illustrations by Drew Frantzen

Library of Congress Cataloging-in-Publication Data

Altea, Rosemary.
   Soul signs : an elemental guide to your spiritual
destiny / Rosemary Altea.
         p.   cm.
   Includes index.
   ISBN-13 978–1–57954–948–0 hardcover
   ISBN-10 1–57954–948–9 hardcover
   ISBN-13 978–1–59486–229–8 paperback
   ISBN-10 1–59486–229–X paperback
   1. Self-actualization (Psychology)—Miscellanea.
2. Typology (Psychology)—Miscellanea.   I. Title.
BF1045.S44A48   2004
131—dc22   2004005320

Distributed to the trade by Holtzbrinck Publishers

2   4   6   8   10   9   7   5   3   1   hardcover
                8   10   9   paperback

We inspire and enable people to improve their lives and the world around them
For more of our products visit **rodalestore.com** or call 800-848-4735

To my own little flower,
God's gift to me.
I will cherish you always.
Your light, your spirit,

Is blinding beauty. . . .
A Visionary Soul,
My one and only child,
Samantha.
Truly my inspiration.

ACKNOWLEDGMENTS

First, my unending gratitude to God, to Grey Eagle, and to the spirit world, for their constancy and continual inspiration. My thanks to my friend and agent, Joni Evans, truly a Bright Star, for her steadfastness, her support, her great advice, and most of all for her enthusiasm and excitement. To my friend and Newborn Soul, Joan, who has spent so many hours working with me on those inevitable and sometimes tedious changes. My thanks also to Denise, the Old Soul, who has worked alongside me and without whose help this book would never have gone beyond the handwritten stage; for her patience and for all her hard work, my many, many thanks. My thanks also to the new little flower in my office, Julliet, definitely the spark of Fire we need to brighten us up. Finally, thanks to my class of students, my willing guinea pigs in this project, and a special thanks to my team of healers in England for their unending friendship and support.

I would also like to thank all at Rodale, from the typesetters to the publicists, the publisher and editors, the mailroom for all the work they are going to be doing, the office staff, and any others I may have missed. My special thanks to Stephanie Tade, who had faith in me and shares my enthusiasm of all things spiritual, and to Chris Potash, the gentle and sensitive genius who helped me put the pieces together. They both, as Water signs, have fed and nourished my Earth-sign nature, and I am overwhelmed.

Also, to my friend and ingenious and innovative Newborn, Marcus Buckingham, my first "reader." His help was invaluable. I will always be grateful.

And finally, to all those who have so graciously and so lovingly taken me to their hearts, I give my thanks, and my love, and my heart, and so, so, so much gratitude.

CONTENTS

PREFACE

This book may seem to be a departure for me, a lighthearted journey into a sort of science of the soul rather than a serious exploration of the spirit world. In fact, my spirit guide, Grey Eagle, led me to this science, and it was he who indicated that it was important that I develop my understanding of this science and explore it. At the heart of it are things called energy groups and soul signs. They are not hard concepts to follow, and they are quite practical. The more you read, the more you know, and in time both make perfect sense.

What may not make sense at first is why I chose to write a book on this subject, with so many "more important" things to write about. Aren't broadcasts from the spirit world, stories of spirit communication, and inspiring stories of healing more critical than delivering this soul mapping that appears (on the surface) to be a type of astrology? Let me explain. I believe that if I can help you unravel the mystery of your soul even a little, then you will have been given the key to open the door to profound personal growth. If we can understand, even a little, why we are here on this earth, we can create meaning in our own lives by making choices that allow us to be better people, that heal us, that give us hope for ourselves and for the world. What could be more important than that?

The knowledge presented in *Soul Signs* can, if we want it to, change our perspective about ourselves, about others, about our relationships, and about our world. It can open our eyes. It can enlighten us. It can help us grow in all the ways we so want to grow.

At each turn in life there are new lessons. Some I miss, and some I grasp. But Grey Eagle has taken great care to teach me patiently about soul signs. Now it is my turn to teach you. I hope you will be as amazed, inspired, and excited as I am when you discover what *Soul Signs* can do for you.

PART ONE

A GARDEN OF SOULS

fire   earth   air   water   sulphur

WALK WITH ME NOW

It was just a little more than five years ago that the subject of soul signs first came up, and the moment Grey Eagle mentioned it to me, I was fascinated. Considering the fact that I have been working with the spirit world for more than twenty years, some of you might find it odd that I hadn't been educated about this important spiritual knowledge sooner. The reason is simple: Until then, I had not been ready, and Grey Eagle knew it. (Nor were any of us, although perhaps some of you have had a glimpse or two.) Since that time I have been an avid and attentive student, learning as much as I can about one of the most fascinating and insightful subjects I have ever been privileged to be involved with, and the greatest thing for me now is that I really get it.

Why was my mother the way she was? Because she was a Fire sign, a Retrospective Soul.

Why does my daughter respond to some situations the ways she does? Because she is an Earth sign, a Visionary Soul.

Why is my sister so easygoing, so different from me? Because she's an Air sign, a Prophet Soul.

How is it that my friend Chris can always find a compromise? Well, she's a Water sign, an Old Soul, and so compromise is easier for her than for others.

And what about you? What kind of soul, what sign are you? As you work your way through this book, you'll find out. You will learn about energy groups, soul signs, clusters, power sources, and energy flow. You will learn about your relationships, about how and why they work or don't work. And as you read you will, I hope, become more and more inspired, as I was, to learn to read the soul signs of others. But first, perhaps I should tell you a little more about myself.

Some of you, I know, have met me before, either through my books or lectures, my Web site, or my work as a spiritual healer. For some of you, though, this will be your first encounter, the first time you have journeyed with me, the first time you have allowed me into your life. Whichever it is, my hope is to inspire you as I have been inspired.

I work in the spiritual realm, teaching, being taught, and trying to grow. My beliefs, as perhaps yours, are simple, and have matured for a variety of different reasons. I believe that we are all souls, a group of souls, on this earth, for who knows what reason . . . and trying to figure it out.

I am perhaps more fortunate than most in that I have Grey Eagle by my side. Grey Eagle came into my life in 1981, and we have been together ever since. I told the story of how we came together in my first book, *The Eagle and the Rose*. As my spirit guide he has helped me find answers to the many questions I have had over the years, sharing his knowledge, his treasures, with me. We are partners: Grey Eagle is the teacher, I am the student. In his time on earth, more than a century ago, Grey Eagle was an Apache shaman, a medicine man, a healer; and so it seems only natural that I too am a healer, with a healing organization based in England and a healing center in Vermont. Grey Eagle helps me in my work and in my life in a variety of ways, and it is his work, and his wisdom, that have led me to the concept of soul signs.

Grey Eagle has always told me that I am a Warrior Soul, and for the longest time I just accepted and never questioned what that might mean. But over the last few years, I began to question; I became more and more intrigued by the possibility of really coming to know about the soul. One of my first questions to Grey Eagle was, "If I am a Warrior Soul, does that mean there are other kinds of souls, and if so . . ." You can imagine that, once begun, the questions were endless. The answers I received have changed the whole way I look at things, at people, at situations, and at all the different kinds of relationships we have. Knowing about soul signs has changed my life, and it can change yours.

From time to time throughout this book I give glimpses of my mediumship, of my ability to communicate with those who have passed. As curious as it sounds, traveling in time and space to other worlds, other dimensions, and returning again and again, then recounting my experiences as best I can, is the gift and the job I was given. It can happen in a heartbeat, unexpectedly, or it can be a controlled and slower process. It can happen in a restaurant, in the street, or at home in my bed. In fact, it can happen anywhere. There are times when I am very aware of it happening, and times when it is so much a part of me that I am unaware.

My friends, those who know me well, know when it is happening. They all describe it the same way: My eyes, they say, seem to move backward, like a slowly turning telescope focusing somewhere beyond their range, as they see me slipping into another world.

I am not aware of this at all, of the movement of my eyes or of any physical changes. For me it has always been, always will be, a natural function of my being. And I like it that way. It means that I can access a place and people some would refer to as invisible. It also means that I can access information, knowledge, and insight that others can't, which doesn't make me all knowing or all seeing by any means, but it does enable me to gain insights and understanding of some of the issues that we mortals find confusing as we struggle with our human existence.

When I first began my work as a spiritual medium, the subjects of life after death and spirit communication, while centuries old, were not nearly as openly talked about as they are today. The very idea of a spiritual medium on a television show . . . "Are you crazy?"

Not so anymore, I'm happy to say. Now we are familiar with these ideas and can explore them freely without producing strange looks, raised eyebrows, or prejudice. As I dip into this unseen realm, I'm searching for pearls, just as a bee goes from flower to flower seeking nectar, seeking food. Each time I go I find a treasure of sorts, a small gem of wisdom I didn't have before. Each time I return I bring back the treasure and add it to my pile. Now here they are, small treasures spilling out onto the pages of this book, ready to be held, each a gem ready to shine out its truth.

All my life I have been used to feeling, seeing, hearing, sensing, intuiting. Understanding how energy works and watching it move, change, and take form comes naturally to me. Explaining it so that you can understand it as well has been my biggest hurdle here. There will be times when I repeat certain key concepts to help you determine your energy group and soul sign with confidence. Stay with me, and trust yourself to intuit your tendencies, your motivations, the real you. I know you'll be glad that you did.

There are so many stories I could tell, enough to fill several books more than I have written already, and each day there are more. My life is rich with the wonder of God and His plan, and all I want to do is share. So come with me now and I will take you on a journey. Walk with me now, and let me tell you about soul signs.

SOME THINGS
WE CAN'T CHANGE,
SOME THINGS WE CAN

Why do I always go for the same kind of partner?
Why does she always fly off the handle?
Why is he always so bossy, always needing to be in control?
Why can't they be more like *me*?
Why can't I be more like *them*?
Why are they the way they are?
Why am I the way I am?

How many times in a week, or even in a day, do we ask these kinds of questions of ourselves? How many times do we get frustrated by someone else's inability to get what we're about, or by our inability to get what someone else is about? Why do we find it so hard to accept people, including ourselves, the way we are?

I wish my mother were more like yours.

I wish my dad were not so moody all the time.

I wish my husband would be more thoughtful and more romantic.

I wish my wife were more affectionate and more giving.

I wish my children were better behaved.

I wish my own childhood had been better.

And on and on, and so it goes—all of us trying to live with one another, all of us trying to live with ourselves, many of us trying to change ourselves or others.

People. People are odd, people are strange, people think differently, act differently, even in the same circumstances. People! Why can't we all behave the same? Why all the conflict, the misunderstanding, the confusion? If we could all come together with one mind, with good intentions, then surely peace would reign in the world. Wouldn't it? Well, couldn't it? So why, after all of our teachings, our wars, our trials, why can't we come to some common understanding? How many times must we marry, be in bad relationships, battle with our children, misunderstand our parents?

Sometimes it seems that no matter how hard we try to change things, we just can't do it. Sometimes we hope that our lives will be different when we wake up tomorrow, that impossible dreams will come true. Often we expect others to behave as we do, or as we think we might, but our expectations are often dashed. We may hope or expect that someone in our life will change, and maybe there are even promises of change, and yet those changes don't happen, or come too little too late. We try to change others, we try to change ourselves, and it doesn't work. We are left wondering: Is there no hope?

Some things are part of our spiritual destiny and we just can't change them: certain instinctive attitudes and impulsive actions, the inability sometimes to act when we know we should, the way we sometimes allow ourselves to be drawn into situations against our better judgment, and, the biggest thing, our reactions—the urge to fight, to shout, to protect, to hide, to dictate, to shrink back, to control, to run. These urges come naturally to us, they are generated by the energy that flows through us and propels us forward. It is energy that dictates our behavior, and no matter how hard we try to control or change it—and there will be times when we can—there will be those times that it will just take us with it and we will not be able to be anything other than who we are.

You may be aware that all beings are made of pure energy, but until now the effects of that energy have never been defined, never been quite understood. We have never really associated a specific type of energy with the way that we think and behave, with what we can and can't change. No one has explored how the unique kind of energy that has powered us since birth makes us tick.

When your soul was first conceived, that initial spark, that crucial moment of creation came from a particular and special source of energy. While the spark is individual to each of us, the type of energy comes from one of five sources: Fire, Earth, Air, Water, or Sulphur. These are the elemental *en-*

ergy groups, the energy sources from which all earthbound souls are created. As your soul was born, it was surrounded by and infused with energy that was present from the beginning of time, without which there would be no creation, no new beginnings. That energy determines what your soul looks like and how it works.

Fire, Earth, Air, Water, or Sulphur—the energy group you belong to gives you your power, your personality, and your character traits. It also provides clues about what kinds of friends and lovers you are bound to be attracted to—and how these relationships might work out over time.

Now you may already be familiar with this concept of the elements from astrology or other ancient disciplines and traditions. Astrology, which involves a study of the stars, has been a fascination to many of us, even if some of us do take it all with a pinch of salt. We are still intrigued, we still want to know. What does the horoscope say today? I'm a Taurean, my daughter is an Aries, and it is fun to know what our star signs say about us and our fortunes. But really, it's more than just fun. You know the old saying, "There are more things to heaven and earth than we can know!"

But while there is a relationship between what you will learn here and other disciplines such as astrology, for the time being, the elemental names—Fire, Earth, Air, and Water—are where the similarities end. For example, my father is astrologically a Pisces, a water sign. His soul sign, however, belongs to the Earth energy group. My mother is an Aquarius, a water sign as well, but her soul sign is imbued with Fire energy. My sister, like my father, is a Pisces, a water sign; her energy group is Air. So even though you may be familiar with astrology signs and their effect on a person's temperament, do not confuse the science of soul signs with astrology. While I believe that all things are connected, and that astrology is just a small area of a vast subject, soul signs tell us so much more about who, why, and what we are.

Fire, Earth, Air, Water, or Sulphur. You *are* one of these five. I *am* one of these five. As we go along together, you will see for yourself which one you are, and what that means.

A person born under the influence of Fire is someone who is instinctively driven by passion, by emotion, sometimes to the point where they will not be able to stop those intense moments of uncontrollable passion and heat no matter how hard they try. To expect them to behave differently would be like trying to stem the flow of an erupting volcano. Impossible.

A person born under the influence of Earth is someone who is instinctively driven by a need to plan and to strategize and who will not, indeed cannot, be anything other than solid and immovable once they have made a decision on a course of action. Expecting them to behave differently would be like expecting a mountain to crumble to dust in front of your eyes. It won't happen.

A person born under the influence of Air is someone who is instinctively driven by a more passive and calming energy flow and will not be able to, nor would they want to, sustain authority over others, as they are generally far too easygoing. To expect someone with a soul sign in the Air group to be different would be the same as expecting the wind to obey your commands— a beyond-rare occurrence.

A person born under the influence of Water is someone who is instinctively driven by a need to evaluate and to compromise, who will be for the most part unable to do anything other than flow with the tide. To try to force them to behave differently would be like standing in the middle of a river and attempting to change its course. It won't work.

There is one more energy group, one other force of nature that drives some of us. This force is unlike the other four. The energy of Sulphur is dark and unwelcoming; a person born under the influence of Sulphur is someone who is instinctively driven by evil, a person who will be both unwilling and also unable to be anything other than dark. To desire love or compassion from such a person, born a dark soul, would be like expecting the most foul-smelling and putrid medicine to taste as sweet as nectar. Never.

So we can see that there are some things we simply cannot change, no matter how hard we try. There are some things we absolutely cannot help.

I was at a seminar recently in New York and was giving a message from the spirit world to a young woman in the audience from her grandmother, who had died from cancer a couple of years before. Part of the old woman's message to her granddaughter was about the younger woman's personal life. She was unhappy, the grandmother told us, and she had threatened several times to leave her boyfriend. It was just not working out. The young woman nodded, tears flowing down her face, acknowledging that her grandmother could see her situation. But did her grandmother have any good advice?

"My granddaughter is a good girl," she told me, "but she's very immature.

She has a bossy nature, and tries to control her boyfriend. You know," she said wisely, "she just can't help it." The daughter clearly was an Earth sign.

Then she went on to tell me that the boyfriend was lovely, a really nice young man, "but he can sometimes be too easygoing, and it drives her crazy." He was definitely an Air sign.

Will she be able to change her controlling nature? As she matures she certainly can, and will, I have no doubt. But there will be times when she will just not be able to stop herself. She just can't help it.

Will her boyfriend change? Of course he can, and will—but only to a point. It's his nature, his energy flow. He's an Air sign. He just can't help it.

Then there are those things that we *can* change—ourselves. For example, Earth signs tend to be bossy or overly assertive and at times can be really difficult to handle. But understanding that they just can't help it can change you. If you are married to an Earth sign, changing your attitude can help you deal with your spouse's challenging character trait in a much more tolerant and understanding way.

Or maybe you have a boss who can be a real pain to work with, as his explosive temper makes you feel inadequate and stupid. Once you realize he's a Fire sign, that he just can't help it, you stop taking it so personally, you stop letting him get to you. You keep your self-esteem, your confidence in you.

Or perhaps you wish your mother would stand up for herself more, but she can't because she's an Air sign. Knowing that she just can't help it, you let go, become more accepting. You stop wishing for the things you cannot change.

Or, as a Water sign you're able to evaluate, to reason, and to compromise, but you wish you were more like your brother, the real action-taker of the family, the one who dares, the one who does. He's a Hunter Soul, an Earth sign, and you, well, you are the more careful and cautious Old Soul. Of course you can't be like him. You just can't help what you are. But when you look at the character traits of each of these two soul signs, you can see that there is just as much value in one as the other. You learn that your strengths come in other ways, other areas, and finally you learn to accept yourself for who you are.

Those things that we can change come from our discovery of ourselves. For our own good, we can change the way we think, the way we feel, and the way we act. Everything is in the attitude.

I am an Earth sign. My daughter, Samantha Jane, is an Earth sign too. But Grey Eagle has told me that I'm a Warrior Soul, while Samantha Jane is a Visionary Soul. In many ways we are so much alike, yet we are different, like two separate varieties of the same flower. For in addition to the five energy groups that propel us in our actions, there are thirteen unique soul signs that determine our personality. Each energy group except Sulphur produces three distinct kinds of souls, and although they all share similarities, by nature they are also very different. Later, as we go into greater detail about each of the soul signs, we will be able to recognize which soul sign we are, and what this means to us.

From the very beginning of your soul's existence, to the present time, and beyond into the future, even into future lives or existences, your soul sign does not change. In other words, I am and have always been a Warrior Soul. In whatever existence I chose to have before this earth life, I was a Warrior Soul. In whatever existence I choose to have after this earth life, I will still, and will always be, a Warrior Soul.

Which of the thirteen soul signs are you?

Fire, Earth, Air, Water, or Sulphur—which energy group is yours?

The world is ready, and so are you. Now you can discover the things you can't change and the things you can, and find out the reasons why.

OUR SOUL:
WHAT IS IT?
WHERE IS IT?

To truly understand our energy group and soul sign, it makes sense that we should find out a little more about how the soul works. We know that we have one, and we pretty much understand that the soul has much to do with our spiritual being. The rest is unclear. As yet, no one has been able to really pin down or to describe what the soul looks like, or to say very much about it that makes it tangible. We've been taught to treasure it, to safeguard it, but the how and what of "it" has remained a mystery . . . until now.

Like many of you, I've known about my soul since I was very young, as my church was my second home, the church elders my family. I was taught to value and to be aware of my soul, that it was my soul that would be saved after my life here on earth was over. I listened, I paid attention, and even though I didn't always understand, I believed. Their teachings were invaluable, and even though my soul was not something I could see or touch, because I trusted my teachers I valued it. Christ was my example, and through that example, my spiritual awakening began. Eventually I learned to listen to the heartbeat of my soul.

Since that time, the time of my youth and my beginnings, I have traveled all over the world and encountered many religious belief systems, some older than Christianity. My eyes were opened to a wider world, a greater experience, and those experiences only increased my faith and made it stronger.

As an extremely inquisitive person, when I see a ghost or apparition, my curiosity overrides any nervousness or fear. "Who are you? What do you want? How can I help you?" I ask. My curiosity simply spills over. Even when I was small, when I was terrified and the fear left me speechless, even then the questions would be in my head. Time and experience taught me to be unafraid, and to be able to voice those questions to the spirit world. And as time has moved on, my questions have become more and more specific.

For the last five years, my questions have been about the soul. What is it? Where is it? Grey Eagle, always ready to teach when I am ready to learn, begins my lesson.

What is our soul?

The soul is our essence, our energy. It is us. Housed for our time on earth within our body, it is able to move in and out of the body at will. Not unlike the brain, our soul holds a wealth of knowledge, many treasures. The soul, our spiritual being, has characteristics, emotions, the ability to learn and to grow, the potential to flower, to mature, and to flourish if we nurture it. It embodies all that we are, all that we have been, and all that we potentially will be.

Using its etheric, or spirit body, the soul can travel the universe and visit with loved ones who have died, and the memories of those visits come through our dreams, dreams that seem so real, but for many, a reality too difficult to grasp. The soul can also visit others on earth, and in my other books you can find examples of this. One example is of a future boyfriend who was brought, by two beings from the spirit world, into my bedroom one night. I saw him clearly and described him in detail to my friends. It was two months later when I met him in the flesh.

Animals also have souls, and are part of our soul cluster, as you will learn later in the book. They play an important role in our earth experience.

At the very beginning of its creation and during its development, the soul, each soul that has ever existed or will in the future exist, is made up of, surrounded by, and influenced by its own particular type of energy coming from a particular elemental energy source. Throughout the universe there are hundreds, if not hundreds of thousands, of energy groups within which a soul can be birthed. On our earth plane, however, only five energy groups exist, groups from which all life is created. All life.

Each of us has the ability to expand that energy, to develop it and use it in many ways. What we cannot change is the type of energy we are. To try to change our energy force is impossible; it would be like trying to turn a chocolate cake into a strawberry shortcake. The ingredients that make up the soul, its power source, will always remain the same—once a Warrior, always a Warrior.

The shape or form of the soul, however, varies with its needs. Almost alienlike, it can become any shape or size it chooses at any given time. It can be as large as the human body which houses it, or it can be as small as the tiniest nerve.

There are moments when our souls talk to one another. Sometimes we are aware of it happening, as when we feel an instant connection with someone. This feeling, negative or positive, is something we instinctively feel. Other times, we may not be consciously aware of such a connection, even though it's there.

In a way, our soul has eyes and ears, it sees, it listens, it pays attention to its experiences. It is we mortals, distracted by material and worldly issues, who need to pay more attention to our soul's energy. The soul determines everything we can be, but we, the mortals, choose much of what we become. By learning about our elemental energy group and our specific soul sign, our soul, we can discover and fulfill our highest destiny.

Where is our soul?

Wherever the soul needs to be, it can be. Housed within the very core of our being, the soul can become the heart, the lungs, the kidney, or the bladder, particularly when one of these organs is in distress and needs a surge of spiritual energy. When we have physical damage—a heart condition, a cancer in the lungs, or a physical disability of any kind—our soul moves in to the affected area to give it power, to give it light and healing. It becomes one with the source of the damage, often creating astonishing results . . . results we call miracles, unexplained healings. There are those of us who feel, during moments of extreme emotional distress, as if something, some presence, is within, calming our emotions. That presence might be of the spirit world, a presence apart from us, or it could be our own soul stirring within us, spreading its energy to those places that need to be healed.

But our soul is also able to travel beyond the human body. It can expand to fill the largest chasm, or contract to become small enough to pass through the eye of a needle. It is free to explore whenever, whatever, and wherever it chooses.

For most people, the soul stays centered within us in our awake time, our conscious time, but as we sleep, as the physical body sleeps, the soul takes the opportunity to stretch, to have its "out" time. Astral travel, dream visions, and out-of-body experiences are examples of the soul's desire to explore. Traveling through time and space, visiting with those in the spirit world, using the etheric body, the spirit body, which is the same size and shape as its physical host, the soul lives and breathes on its own, just as it has a mind and a will of its own.

Although it can travel far and wide, the soul remains joined to our physical body by a thin silver thread until that moment of complete separation when the cord breaks and we are no longer of this earth.

We, as souls, chose to be here on earth, to have this earth experience. Yes, chose, which might be hard to believe for those who have had a difficult life. Why would we choose this? The reason is simple: learning, growth, expansion, knowledge. But why? Again, simple. Our souls must flourish or they will wither away and die, and so our earth experience is our school, our opportunity to learn and grow, and with unlimited potential.

In Greek mythology, the handsome young man Narcissus fell in love with his own reflection and was turned into a flower by the gods, to gaze into the water at himself forever. Like Narcissus, by figuring out our soul sign we are able to gaze at our own soul's reflection, to reflect on who and what we are, and what we might become during our earth experience.

That is how our soul is, just like a flower bulb, like a daffodil. The soul enters the human body coming from a variety of places within the universe, going to those waiting stations, transportation fields, which take it through the many tunnels and force fields, to arrive safely at its chosen destination, poised and ready for its new life. The roots of the soul, that part of the soul that feeds it, spread out and bury themselves deep down within the physical body. By feeding on our life experiences, the soul gains nourishment and begins to flourish. The bulb is nurtured, and the flower blooms.

Naturally, once we understand this, we want to know how to nurture our soul to make it bloom to its full potential. What is it that we need to do, and what exactly does the growth of our soul mean? Does it mean that we should be better people, do more for others, be more spiritual? Of course, and like many of you, I have tried, struggled and strived, failed and succeeded, but so often in my desire to grow, I feel that I'm in the dark, blundering along like a blind man without a cane.

The growth of our soul . . . As I learned more about soul signs, the meaning of the phrase became clear. I, my soul, must find fulfillment, self-knowledge; I must expand my energy, open myself up to all things, learn to be unafraid. Then I will flourish, like the bulb which has been nurtured, cared for, fed, and watered. My soul will bloom, and my flower, my spirit, will be the brightest and the most beautiful thing, and I will see myself as a being of light.

Soul signs. I opened myself up, and here is what Grey Eagle taught me. The student was ready. The teacher began.

"You are a Warrior Soul, born to the universe a long, long time ago, born before ever you came to this earth plane. I too am a Warrior Soul, born to the universe more than a long, long time ago. I am a soul who is more grown, more mature than you, but still I am a Warrior soul, still with all the traits that a Warrior soul has."

For a moment I was filled with pride. A Warrior Soul, how great, how incredible . . . Wasn't it? It seemed to be, it sounded like it, but it took a while before I asked, "What is a Warrior Soul?"

As I went down this new path, struggling to understand, naturally I asked about my daughter. Was Samantha Jane a Warrior Soul too? Grey Eagle told me no, that she was different than me, a different bulb, a different bloom, and here on earth for reasons other than mine, and meant to flower in a very different way. That was easy for me to understand, because although in many respects we are very much alike, in others my daughter and I are indeed very different. My next question to Grey Eagle was, "If Samantha is different than me, does that mean that we are all different? And if we are, what is it that makes those differences?"

Soon I began learning about the five elemental groups, five different sources of energy. I learned about soul signs, thirteen in all, and wondered why there were so few. It was at this point I learned about soul clusters. "A cluster," I heard Grey Eagle say, "you are all part of a soul cluster. All souls who have a life experience on the earth plane are part of the same soul cluster. All alike in so many ways, connected, bonded by your like-nesses, yet each one very different also. This is how it is, and this is how you are."

Although I'm not too familiar with astronomy, I do know a little about star clusters, groups of stars that are close to each other in space and re-semble each other in certain characteristics, which implies a common origin. A star within a star cluster always has one or more of the same char-acteristics of the other stars in its cluster. All stars in the same cluster move at the same rate and in the same direction. Some common clusters are the Seven Sisters; the Sailboat, located in the Milky Way; the Hyades; and the Praesepe. Most of us have gazed at these star clusters, or constellations, from time to time.

So, a star cluster is a group of stars, each one with at least one common characteristic, all moving at the same rate, all going in the same direction.

But how does that relate to us? What, exactly, is a soul cluster?

Well, those souls here on earth, we mortal beings, are in many ways so alike, though it would seem to me that we do move at a different rate from one another and we definitely seem to go in many different directions at once, which is part of the confusion and also part of the excitement of being human. But Grey Eagle tells me that it is our planet, Earth, which moves, and as it does, all of us move along with it at the same rate, and yes, of course, in the same direction. He tells me that within the universe there are many, many soul clusters, groups of souls having experiences in places other than the earth plane. However, for we mortal beings, our soul cluster consists of five groups, five primary sources of energy, thirteen varieties of souls in all.

Unseen, and before now having no conceptual tangible form, each soul is here for the same reason, each on a journey of discovery. So what happened to us, why did we become so mindless of our soul, of our spiritual nature, so mindless of our spiritual needs? Technology happened, science happened, a new and changing and incredibly exciting world, filled with tangibles, that's what happened. We learned to embrace the "I see," we were wowed by it, like children at the most spectacular fireworks display. So in awe of the tangibles, we were, that we forgot the "I don't see"s "I can't see"s—the intangibles. We learned to want more, to want bigger, better, and over time the intangibles, the soul, the spirit, became less important. Like the old adage goes, "Out of sight, out of mind."

Many of us began to remember God only in moments of despair, confusion, or loss. Only in those tragic or traumatic moments are we silent long enough to hear the quiet calling of our inner spirit, and only in those moments do we feel the steady aching of our neglected soul.

There is a mix of sadness and joy as our earth becomes more and more in turmoil, and terrifying things are happening, as the age of science and technology shows its teeth. The monster, that spectacular fireworks display we have for years marveled at, is turning into a dragon of fire that threatens to consume us, and to destroy the very things we have valued most: life, success, progress.

In the old days, in the days of trolls and fairy tales, there was always one hero who would try to slay the dragon. Unfortunately, the dragon of our modern day is not one creature, one being, but a collective mentality: the collective mentality of the human race, which chose to enter into a race for more, for bigger, for better, for power, for everything, feasting on greed and never sated. Even the most humble of us becomes tempted by the menu our race has created. Even the most spiritual of us is vulnerable to temptation, for after all, our common characteristics, our common link, is that we are only human, and fallible.

Now the world is turning once again, it is changing, we are changing. I feel it, and I trust my feelings. I have faith, and I trust my faith. As I write, I look to Grey Eagle and his eyes tell me that I am right. Our world is not coming to an end, only the world as we know it. The change has been taking place for some time, and now so many of us are asking who, and what, and why. We are finally ready to acknowledge once again that we are so much more than human beings living a human existence. And the joy is that we want it this way, we are beginning to know the value of our spirit, of our souls, once more.

The dragon that the human race has created will not be slayed, nor indeed does it need to be, and this makes me unafraid, unafraid for the world, for my child, and for myself. We need our science, our technology, because when used in a good way we all benefit greatly. But we must harness and make harmless all that endangers our society, and each of us must take responsibility for that. Those of us who know this, who recognize the power of the soul, and that each of us can make a difference, will join forces, and together we will put out the dragon's fire.

So, what is it, where is it? We come back to the beginning, back to the questions we first asked, to pin down the intangible and make it a substantial and real entity.

Our soul is like the daffodil bulb, not necessarily the same shape but with clear similarities. Burying its roots deep into the earth, deep in the core of us, it seeks out all that can nourish it. Becoming nourished, certain things happen, the process not unlike a flowering bulb, and when the food, the compost, is good, and when the climate in which it grows is right, then the soul flourishes. If its nourishment is not good, or if the compost is inadequate, which happens through neglect or negative deeds, thoughts, and actions, then the bulb, the soul, will become small and shriveled and will either have a small and pathetic-looking bloom or will simply not flower at all.

When we remember the bloom of the daffodil bulb, we can immediately visualize that bright yellow trumpet standing tall and proud amongst its fellows, for rarely do you see a single daffodil.

In British gardens especially, the daffodil is a favorite. Native to Britain and Europe since the Ice Age, a garden is not a garden without a multitude of these yellow flowers, planted in clusters to fill the borders. I remember vividly the gardens of the house I grew up in. My father, when he retired from the army, became an ardent gardener, and he filled his garden with old English flowers, peonies, foxgloves, roses of course, poppies and Michaelmass daisies, irises and delphiniums, and masses more. Spring was the most breathtaking time of all. A profusion of daffodils, too many to count, too many almost to imagin . . . and as I write, my soul takes me back in time to a place where I was young and full of hope.

From the street and through the small gate. Four steps down and along the narrow path by the side of the house to the tall gate, at least seven feet high. Lift the latch and open the gate and . . . into wonderland. The gray of the world left behind, I remember the gold of the garden, a thousand and more of the most perfect trumpet blooms, swaying, moving in unison, like golden waves on a gentle sea, crowded together and supporting each other, just as we all should do. As a child, and as a young woman, I experienced each spring the same, never failing to make time stand still. It was magical.

When I remember those childhood moments, I can't help but wonder: Did my soul call out to me, to try to tell me something? Did I hear it? Did I hear the heartbeat of my soul? I don't know, I simply can't remember. But I do remember that the magic of that host of daffodils never failed to touch me, and the memory touches me still.

The soul, like the daffodil bulb, strives to reach its potential, to flower. The soul's bloom, its resulting energy, is what we call the spirit, our spirit. As we feed our soul, the aura or energy field of the soul gains light, brilliant yellow light. The more good nourishment the soul receives, the more attention, the bigger and brighter its aura, its flower, becomes. The bulb blossoms, the soul blooms, its incredible energy and the light that it brings enable the soul to see more clearly, to grow more strong, and like the daffodil it is a cycle, never ending; even when life on earth has ended, still the cycle of life continues on.

Now we see the soul as a tangible thing. A special and rare bulb. This is how it is. This is who we are. And we must treat it as the most important and delicate gift. Visualize planting your bulb in the richest of soil, as you would with any rare bulb, and try placing it in the most compatible and best of environments. Do not feed it poisons, bad thoughts, or negative actions, but give it only the nourishment that will benefit it most: kindness, gentleness, and love. Be the gardener of all gardeners as you tend your bulb and wait for it to flower.

As we progress to the next chapters and learn more about our energy groups and our soul signs and learn how to recognize ourselves, we will see more of the daffodil and its similarities to us, to our soul, no longer such a mystery, now a tangible thing. And we will know that each of us, each soul, although separate and individual, is joined together as a soul cluster, united by our common needs, and never alone. What a fabulous garden we make. Each one of us a flower. A flower in a garden of souls.

AS ALL GOOD GARDENERS KNOW

The soul's growth process and its struggle for knowledge can be a difficult thing. Hard to define, but not impossible to achieve, the learning process of the soul depends on many things.

Like the daffodil bulb, which requires a good hard frost in order to germinate, so the soul needs the same. A good hard frost, which often comes in the form of a trauma or tragedy of some kind, will often mark the beginning of the soul's ability to mature.

Maturity doesn't have a great deal to do with cranial knowledge, but it has everything to do with our use of that knowledge. This is why, prior to our birth here on this earth, it is of paramount importance that we must be placed in the right environment for our earthly experience, so that we gain the maximum benefit, have the widest possible range of opportunities from that experience.

Where we are born, to whom we are born, and how we are born are all decided before our birth, and are all very important to our growth potential. Each of these decisions is carefully decided by that higher power, by God, by our angels and our guides, weighed carefully in order to give us the best chance of reaching our potential, of obtaining some degree of growth, fulfillment, and enlightenment. We are given many tools with which to work throughout our mortal experience, tools which we will take with us after our earth life is complete.

As all good gardeners know, if you want your flowers to bloom well, take time and pick the spot carefully before you plant. God, as we know, is the best of gardeners, and His interest is in seeing His garden of souls bloom to their fullest and best. His hand is in everything around us, and we only have to look to see that all we need in life is right at our fingertips.

As we souls weigh our needs, our wants, our goals, prior to birth here, we do not do so alone. There are many souls who guide us in this process, more mature than we, our teachers, our guides, our angels, who help us make the right choices. But ours is the final choice; we are the ones who make the final decisions.

So, bearing in mind the opportunities we are seeking, and that we do so for our soul's growth, some of us may choose to have the experience of good family, loving parents, and a good education. Some souls may choose just the opposite; they may choose to have difficult and traumatic experiences that can push them to the limits of their abilities. Whatever choice we make, that choice is based on advancing our soul's maturity. We are seeking to be enlightened. This is our goal, and even those souls who come to earth already mature prior to their existence here will often deliberately place themselves in a difficult environment in order to fulfill themselves further.

Many souls leave this earth having only partially achieved their goals. A few will leave here having achieved almost nothing. And there will be others who will have reached their goals, surpassed those goals, and who reach a higher state of enlightenment than they imagined existed for them. In maturity it is possible to advance so much here on this earth, and to be of such great help to those souls who, floundering a little in their quest to bloom, will reach out a willing and needy hand for help.

So, where we are born matters. To whom we are born matters. And how we are born also matters. It is important to know what soul signs our parents are, what soul signs our siblings and our aunts and uncles are. What soul signs, what forces of nature surround us? How will those forces influence us? How will we allow them to influence us? How will we influence them? Which of our positive and negative traits will we exercise most as we struggle to grow?

If you have a parent who shows spite toward you, it will always be your choice how to respond. Our soul knows this, you know this, we all know this. It is true, however, that we have lost touch with the truth of our purpose, and often feel baffled and bewildered by the seeming happenstance and hard luck of our lives. By acknowledging not only that we have a purpose, but that it is one we chose before birth, you are given the power to make the most of your life. Teasing out where your soul's choices begin and end, and where the effects of our environment begin and end, can be enormously complex and fascinating. When you begin the process of determining your energy group and soul sign, you'll find that distinction challenging. Yes, the "figuring out" is an important part of learning to know yourself. Working with others, determining what part of their character is their soul, and what is the result of the effects of the world on their personality, will teach you compassion and empathy. And if you have lost touch or even refused to acknowledge this until now, the new awareness has the power to open up a whole new world to you.

Learned behavior plays an important part in our growth process, and as it is by design that we were born into our particular environment, our particular soul system, our family, we must acknowledge that there are many solid and good reasons for this.

Through our interactions with other souls, with other soul signs, especially when we are young, we are given many opportunities . . . and choices. In our formative years, when we are so innocent, open, and easily influenced, our positive and negative experiences leave impressions on us, and throughout our lives our actions and reactions are greatly influenced by those experiences. But as we grow, and even from a very early age, we are making choices. We know what is wrong behavior, and we know what is right behavior. Our soul, through seeing and listening, feeling and thinking, makes determinations and tells us so. We feel them as instincts. And then we choose. We choose how to be and how not to be. We choose which character traits to exercise positively, and which ones to exercise negatively.

There are many differing viewpoints on nature versus nurture, and there are those who believe that bad behavior can be excused and understood if a person doesn't know better. The theory that someone who has been abused as a child will go on to abuse their own children, and so on, because they don't know differently is widely held. But children do know. We all know.

Learned behavior. When a child is abused, he or she knows, even as it is happening, that it is wrong. I knew. I was abused. When a child is treated unfairly in any way, he or she knows that it is wrong. I knew. I was treated unfairly. And when a child is treated with love and affection, he or she knows that it is right. I knew. I saw how other kids were treated with love and affection by their parents. I knew. My soul cried out to me and told me so. We all know. We all know right from wrong. Our souls cry out to us and tell us so. And we decide, we make our choices, and we are responsible for those choices. We, no one else but we, decide.

Anger, hurt, pain, humiliation, fear, dread, confusion—all these emotions we choose. Do we hold on to our anger, our pain and humiliation, and hit back, or do we strive to understand that we can do better?

I was about twenty-four years old the time I came through the garden gate to the sound of a small child sobbing in fear and confusion outside the back door of the house I grew up in. It felt like I'd been punched in the stomach, and for a fleeting moment it was me standing there, I was the girl, sobbing and afraid.

The door was suddenly flung open, and my sister and mother, laughing, calling the child a crybaby, threw a bucket of cold water all over her, and collapsed, giggling hysterically into each other's arms as the child screamed and spluttered uncontrollably.

In a flash, I scooped the child up into my arms. At the same time, in a voice deadly calm and quiet, I turned on my mother and sister and said,

"What in God's name do you think you're doing?" Guilt, knowing, anger, indignation—I saw all of these emotions on my mother's face. She had been caught out, and she didn't like it. In my sister's eyes I saw shame, only shame, for she knew what she had done was wrong. Trying to please her mother, desperately needing her mother's love and approval, as we all do, she had become her mother and betrayed her child. But she knew it was wrong, and the choice to play the game had ultimately been hers.

A thousand good reasons don't make one good excuse for bad behavior. Of course, we are affected by our upbringing, and our behavior patterns are influenced greatly by our childhood experiences. But our inborn energy, the power we have, our soul's character traits, how we use our power, and how we develop and exercise our character traits—this is what makes us who we really are.

Nature versus nurture: My sister moved away from my mother's neighborhood and, less influenced by my mother's powerful and negative nurturing, her true nature, the wonderful character traits of her Prophet Soul, began to develop. She blossomed and became a really great mom. She always knew right from wrong. She always had choices, but sometimes she didn't feel strong enough to exercise them in the best way.

We need to remember that each of us is a flower, a small flower in a garden chosen for us by God, surrounded by other flowers, most of us like the daffodil. There are thirteen soul signs, twelve of them golden bright flowers, shining spirits that are of God; the thirteenth, a dark flower, just one among the rest of us, one soul sign of evil intent.

We, in our human form, our souls so much like the daffodil bulb, we need that good hard frost, that trauma which gives us our growth spurts.

Often, though, what we learn through trauma we forget as life goes on. So our soul requires yet another hard frost, and then another—a good hard shock, so often necessary for our growth.

It is easy, in retrospect, for most of us to see our mistakes. The hard part comes in remembering, and in making our corrections. And as all good gardeners know, a beautiful garden, with perfect and lovely blooms, can only be achieved through trial and error, and a lot of hard work.

PART TWO

ENERGY GROUPS

fire   earth   air   water   sulphur

AND THEN THERE ARE FIVE

Getting to know our own energy group and soul sign and then the soul signs of our families and friends is both fun and practical. When we look at the compatibility of each of the soul signs, we will see which soul types we can have a real connection with and which we probably cannot. We will see where clashes of personality are likely to occur, and where strong bonds of friendships can easily take place. Before we go on, though, let's take a closer look at how our soul cluster is divided into its various energy groups.

In the universe there are many sources of energy from which beings are created, but those souls who at some point in their creation are earthbound, even if only momentarily, as in the case of an unborn fetus or stillborn child, these are created from one of the earth's five elemental energy groups.

Let's take a look again at these five energy sources, the soul's power supply, and see if we can immediately recognize which one "is us."

Our first group, created from the energy of Fire, is comprised of those individuals who are driven and propelled by their emotions. Influenced by a powerful and sometimes hard-to-control energy, the individual born of Fire is likely to be somewhat uncompromising and willful, but also passionate, fascinating, creative, and challenging. *The Fire energy group of souls is driven by and acts through their emotion.*

Our second group, created from the energy of Earth, is influenced by an energy that is powerful, though sometimes hidden beneath the surface. Earth energy produces an individual who is sometimes misunderstood and underestimated by others, who will be resourceful even when they are most afraid, and, most of all, who is compelled to take action. *The Earth energy group of souls is driven by and acts through planning and strategizing.*

Coming to our third group, created from the energy of Air, we have those who are influenced by an energy so seemingly unobtrusive that it might go unnoticed. A strong energy, yet quietly so, calm and gentle, it manifests in individuals who are easygoing if somewhat passive or passive-aggressive, and who feel a need to please. *The Air energy group is driven by and acts through frustration or oppression.*

Group four, created from the energy of Water, includes individuals with a strong sense of fairness and the ability to compromise, who thrive on peace and harmony, and who like everyone to be happy. *The Water energy group is driven by and acts through evaluation and compromise.*

Our fifth and final group, created from the energy of Sulphur, is the Dark Soul. Unlike the other four groups, each one producing three clearly individual soul signs, the Dark Soul has only one sign, although there are three different degrees of this energy. This soul emits energy that is without light and is devoid of God. It is consumed by evil and feeds on pain, fear, and destruction. *The Sulphur energy group is driven by and acts through a desire to corrupt.*

The majority of us relate to the first four groups, and we immediately want to know more. The fifth group is so scary, we might want to ignore its existence. But we can't. Are there really such souls? Yes, this pocket of souls is part of our soul cluster and has had a major influence on all of us, so it must be included. Being part of a soul cluster means that we each have one or more of the traits of the other souls in that cluster, but what same or similar trait could the rest of us possibly have with the Dark Soul?

Ill will toward others? Even the most spiritually inclined are capable of that. Spite? I hear the word and cringe. Although I don't like to admit it, I know that even the best of us can be spiteful sometimes, maybe most in childhood. I know I can be. . . . And a few painful memories flash across my mind.

When I was in elementary school, there was a girl in my class who, I must admit, I really didn't like. I can't remember her name, but I can easily remember what she looked like.

I had a boyfriend whose name was Anthony Booth, and we loved each other as only six- and seven-year-olds can. He was my knight in shining armor, and he protected me and cared for me until, at age twelve (I was eleven), he moved to another school, away from the area.

Now, Anthony Booth was never unfaithful, never looked at another girl, and always shared his Bluebird licorice toffees only with me. Of that I'm sure. He would sneak them from a jar in his mother's living room from time to time. Always two. One for him, and one for me.

The girl I disliked, more and more it seemed, each day, also liked Anthony Booth, and flirted with him at every opportunity while at the same time telling me she was going to be his girlfriend one day, not me.

Red hair. She had very red hair, which was long and always in beautiful ringlets. She would boast and brag that her mother set it in rags every night, and she would come into school with her shining curly red hair, her nice dresses, black patent shoes, and try to steal away my boyfriend.

Did I feel ill will toward her? You bet I did. Spite and envy, that's what I felt. I had no self-esteem, and felt small and inadequate—my first memory of having these feelings, though unfortunately not my last.

Had I been a Fire sign, driven by my emotions, I might have acted, kicked out in anger. As an Earth sign, though, I had not yet dared to assert my true nature, that of the Warrior. But I learned—and I learned how to kick back with the greatest effect, to use that small dark energy within me, that small dark part of my soul, to hurt back if someone hurt me or my child.

Another memory . . . My very best friend had an affair with my husband, the details of which are too sordid and unnecessary to tell. At first I was too hurt and felt too betrayed, more by her than by him, to take any kind of action at all. Her husband called and asked if it was true. I said no, feeling that one marriage was already destroyed, one person already deeply hurt. I saw no reason to cause more hurt and pain, especially to him.

A little time passed, my husband returned home, and we resumed our way of life as best we could. But each day when I picked my daughter up from school, *she* was there. I would hide in the car and watch as she chatted and laughed with the other mothers. No sense of shame, or guilt; no apparent feelings of humiliation, as I had.

Weeks passed, and I began to plan, to strategize, to figure out a way to pay her back. I fantasized about mowing her down with the car, and once or twice came pretty close to doing it. Something stopped me, but I had been forced onto the battlefield, and if I was indeed going to draw my sword, I was also going to make sure I drew blood. So I waited. I plotted. I planned. I watched as she mingled with the other mothers, her life going on as before.

Then one day, instead of hiding in the car, embarrassed and ashamed, I got out and strode up to the school gates. She saw me coming, and I saw the fear in her face. It comforted me, it gave me purpose. I stood behind her, close enough for her to feel my breath on her neck, and I jiggled my keys . . . just to make sure that she knew I was coming after her.

Day after day, week after week, at the school gates, in the grocery store, anywhere I saw her, I would stand behind her and jiggle my keys, each time making her afraid, each time drawing blood. . . . Her fear was palpable. So too was my strength, and indeed, my spite. I wanted to make her suffer as she had made me suffer. Did I know it was wrong? Yes, I did. Did I care? No. It was only later that I felt ashamed, and then, in truth, only just a little bit.

There are other stories, other examples I could recount of when I felt the need to hurt, to strike out, to intentionally hurt someone else, but a thousand reasons do not make one good excuse. Still, it is that strong urge to hurt, to harm, which is our common link to the Dark Soul.

As children, our actions born of spite and envy are limited. As adults, there are no boundaries we cannot cross—if we choose. And every one of us has that trait within us, to a lesser or greater degree.

So although I am not generally a spiteful or envious person, in certain circumstances, at certain moments in my life, I am capable of those feelings.

We all are. And when they occur, no matter how brief the moment, a small part of our soul becomes dark. The bulb is bruised, the spirit, the flower, becomes, for a moment, damaged, and the bloom is made less perfect.

One of the great things about the soul, however, is its resilience. As long as it has a little food and water, attention, and care, it survives. The damage we do to it through neglect, negativity, or simple ignorance can be repaired. The more good nourishment we give to the soul, the bigger and brighter its bloom becomes.

We all want to flower, to be strong, and bright, and beautiful, like the daffodil. We all want to grow and we all want to make a better life for ourselves. That's why we're here. Some of us put more effort into it than others; some of us simply don't know how. Knowing which energy group, which pocket of energy we belong in gives us a start, it gives us an understanding we didn't have before as to why, how, and for what reasons we think, feel, act, and react. Every one of us is aligned with one of these five elemental sources of energy; there are no exceptions. We are all connected, we all affect one another. Let's take a closer look at how.

IT'S ELEMENTAL

We see the forces of nature at work all the time, in one way or another. From the smallest and most fragile leaf of a plant as it forces its way up through dry, hard-packed earth, to the volcano that lies dormant for years and then suddenly roars and rumbles and spits out its fire. These are the dramatic forces of nature we all know well. We also know about those forces of nature that are ever present but unseen, or should I say not so obviously at work. The planet turns, though we don't feel it move; clouds form, too high for us to notice their existence—the beginnings of a storm before it breaks; the sun blazes on, even during our earthly night.

When we think of our own energy, it can be hard to grasp how powerful a force each of us is. In nature, the effects of energy are much more obvious. Earthquakes, tornadoes, hurricanes, El Niño and El Niña—all these events produce tangible, if destructive, results. Within the human race, within our soul cluster, our energy is not so obvious but just as powerful and driving. In fact, we souls are affected and propelled by these same natural forces, these same powerful elements: Fire, Earth, Air, Water, and Sulphur.

Which one are you?

As you read the descriptions of each group again, you might seem to fit into more than one. When I heard the description of the Earth sign, I knew it was me. Then I read the description of the Water sign, and that too seemed to be me. As the Earth sign and the Water sign have a lot in common, both needing to evaluate situations, both able to stand back, to figure things out calmly and unemotionally, my confusion was not surprising. I seemed to fit both, but not really. The influence of Earth energy means that when all the evaluating and strategizing are done, an action of some sort is demanded. The influence of Water is different. Yes, they plan, they strategize, but unlike our Earth signs, an action is not always necessary, except the action of compromise. And too much evaluating, which our Water signs can be prone to, often results in nonaction. Earth signs are proactive, they need action. Water signs do not. Another thing that rules me out as a Water sign is that although I am often willing to compromise, it is not my natural inclination; I have to work at it. So although I can behave in so many ways just like the other groups, my need to plan *and* act places me securely as an Earth sign.

One of my students first thought she was an Air sign, as she saw herself as passive and pliable. Yet as she read the description of the Fire sign, it too resonated. Which was she, maybe a little of both? Yes, of course, as part of the earth soul cluster we all have a little in us of each energy. But what my student eventually realized is that her perceived passivity was more a repression of her emotions. Through behavior learned over many years, she had developed the ability to supress her feelings, to store them inside. But this had been a struggle, as her passionate nature was always simmering under the surface. She is definitely a Fire sign.

What we have to do is look at what it is that drives us to take action. Is it passion? Is it planning? Is it frustration or oppression? Is it a need to find ways to make things work through compromise?

Let's look again at the five energy groups, this time in a little more detail, and see if we can become clearer on our own energy force.

FIRE. Passion and emotion can be as obvious as the brightest flame, or as unobtrusive as coals nestled in a bank of ash. Loud, crackling, with sparks flying, or inwardly and quietly simmering, passionate, always with the potential to burst out, exciting, creative, sometimes controlled, sometimes not. Warmhearted, extremely sensitive, spirited, impassioned, compulsive, bright and blazing, mysterious and moody, or inwardly burning with inspiration. Influenced by and acting through emotion.

Is this you?

EARTH. Earth signs are planners and strategists. They have an innate sense of groundedness. Realistic and able to rationalize, rock solid and reliable, practical and sensible, inwardly having a hard core, a depth of reasoning that goes beyond emotions and allows for concrete and objective thinking. Influential, intentioned, always ready to take action, supportive, safe, and often possessing timely, groundbreaking, and innovative ideas. Always productive, with a sense of fair play and right intention. Generally focused and instinctive.

Is this you?

AIR. Air signs are passive, dislike conflicts, are able to rise above the turmoil and angst of the world, except in those moments of updraft or downdraft, when currents of deep emotion might cause a swift and unexpected reaction, sometimes, although rarely, in the proportions of a monsoon or tornado, quick to come and quick to go. Generally easygoing, easily inspired, able to go with the flow, light and cheerful, able to float, adapting to most situations and circumstances without fuss, mostly open, what-you-see-is-what-you-get, hopeful of people and outcomes, trusting, and gentle. Acts only when driven by frustration or held down by oppression.

Is this you?

WATER. Water signs are signs of navigation and detour, able to coast along or be forceful, fluid and easygoing, waters running deep, which means deep emotions and needs can become submerged, swamped, or waterlogged in certain situations. Able to flow, to move with the tide, to find a way around things, to follow the natural course or flow of energy rather than battle against it, ebbing and flowing, winding and rippling, capable of bubbling or floating, always trying to move on a steady course.

Is this you?

SULPHUR. The last group in our cluster of souls is the sign of sulphur, a foaming, wrathful, and enraging energy. Whether hidden or obvious, always smoldering, sizzling, or just plain boiling, clever and cunning or obviously incensed and violent, this is a torrid force that is passionately and angrily demonic and, indeed, damned.

Is this you?

At this point, you should have a pretty good idea of your energy group, but for those of you still not sure, see which group of statements below resonates most with you.

- You sometimes have regrets, but nonetheless you revel in the joy of having created an effect, whether good or bad. You live in a drama of sorts, either emotionally or creatively.

- You are a person who needs attention, who needs to be recognized and admired, who is sensitive and easily hurt over the smallest thing, who can love and hate with equal passion.

- You are a person who thrives on love and passion in personal relationships, who needs to be number one in their partner's life, who likes to have their own way, who feels easily neglected and is capable of being quite jealous when their spouse's attention is somewhere else.

If these describe you, then you are a **Fire sign**.

- You are a person who needs to plan before acting, although you are determined to turn your plans into action. You make lists and like to take control.

- You pay close attention, striving for perfection, even in the little things, generally organized, especially in situations you consider important, sensitive but able to reason and to be fair, steady, and reliable.

- You thrive on being the organizer in the family; are loyal to your spouse and expect the same respect and loyalty in return; can seem on occasion to be bossy and you like to take charge; you like to be romanced and need genuine affection.

If these describe you, then you are an **Earth sign**.

- You don't like pressure, and you don't like to be upset or argue, but you do like new people and new experiences.

- You love animals and children, do not sweat the small stuff, and are usually easygoing, happy to go along in life without fuss, generally calm, and somewhat passive.

- You thrive on simply being loved, are undemanding in your personal relationships, like to keep things simple and uncomplicated, hate arguments and fights, and will try in most cases with your spouse to pacify and keep things on an even keel.

If these describe you, then you are an **Air sign**.

- You usually find a way, through compromise, to please others and yourself. You are able to evaluate and solve problems by negotiating and seeking harmony.
- You avoid attention, shy away from the limelight but still like approval from others for work well done; you strive to be fair and considerate of others' feelings, but can be so immersed in your own life that you can be neglectful of issues outside yourself or your family.
- You thrive on the ability to communicate with your spouse and family; feel the need to always strive to be seen to be reasonable, even when they perhaps cannot be; and are strong-minded and capable of standing your ground in an argument when issues are important.

If these describe you, then you are a **Water sign**.

- You love the idea of being disruptive and creating disharmony in any and every circumstance.
- You demand attention, become angry and vengeful when it is not given, and plan to get even with those who do not do your bidding.

You ignore others' needs and wants and are concerned only with your own needs.

- You do evil deeds, think evil thoughts, feel evil passions, and will use your spouse, your family, and any and all relationships in whatever way you want without regard for others.

If these describe you, then you are a **Sulphur sign**.

As you read, keep in mind that this is not about what you would like to see yourself as but the real you. Other than the fifth group, which most of us are not, don't be afraid that one group is better, more powerful, or more desirable than another. Each of the four primary groups has equal merits. Each is desirable in its own way. I am glad to be an Earth sign, but I'm so grateful for my friends and colleagues who are those Fire, Air, and Water signs. Life would be boring if we were all the same, and our learning potential would be very limited.

ACTING IN AND OUT
OF CHARACTER

None of us is isolated. We have family, friends, and colleagues who all belong to their own energy groups. We are constantly surrounded by different types of energy, which overflow into one another, sometimes connecting well, sometimes clashing. Each of us is affected by the energy of others; our soul's character traits can be disturbed and disrupted, increased or depleted. All of us are capable sometimes of acting out of character, especially if we allow ourselves to be overly influenced by another's stronger energy flow.

We can all act like a Fire sign and allow our emotions to get the better of us: exploding in temper, lashing out, or acting spontaneously, feeling driven to give someone an unexpected hug, to show our emotions.

The young woman, an Earth sign, usually in control of her emotions, is given a surprise twenty-first birthday party. She bursts into tears at the unexpected pleasure. Caught off guard, she displays her inner feelings. Our Air sign, usually passive, explodes in temper when some incompetent driver comes out of a side road without warning and rams into her brand-new car. Or our Water sign, usually evaluating how to spend that hard-earned check, spontaneously splurges on that great pair of shoes which she just can't help but buy, unable to resist that urge . . . that emotion.

We all show our emotions to some degree or another, but it is only Fire signs who are naturally driven to act by the energy force of their emotions, whose emotions, first and foremost, dictate their actions. That is their main characteristic, and most of the time they behave in character. We are all capable of planning and strategizing, as our Earth signs do automatically, even though we may not be good at it. If a Fire sign is going through a really messy divorce, her emotions will definitely be bubbling away under the surface and even spilling over, but she is more than capable of setting aside those emotions to plan, to strategize, when it is crucial.

Likewise, Air signs are very capable of planning and strategizing if something is important enough to them. However, because they are naturally driven by that passive energy force, they may feel quite guilty if their plans affect someone else adversely. Water signs come the closest in their natural ability to plan and strategize as Earth signs do, although this is not the energy that drives them to action. More than capable of planning that trip of a lifetime and making sure that every detail has been taken care of, they are still likely to closely evaluate their routes and will take action only after considering everything carefully. Determined and immediate action does not come as naturally to them.

Planning, strategizing, and taking action does not come as easily to the other groups as it does to our Earth sign. It is more uncharacteristic of them.

And yes, every one of us is capable of passive behavior, which is the natural inclination of an Air sign, but for Fire and Earth signs it can be much more of a struggle, and they will do it only when they tell themselves they must. Water signs find it easier because, like Air signs, they are generally easygoing, they naturally give and take. A Water sign, setting out to the movies, is much more inclined to let their partner choose the film. Fire and Earth signs would be much more inclined to voice their preference.

There is a little of the Water sign in all of us, I think: the desire to compromise, the ability to evaluate. But not all of us are good at it, especially, once again, Fire and Earth signs. Earth signs do have a distinct ability to reason and evaluate, but compromise is not what drives them. Compromise would be uncharacteristic.

The energy of Sulphur is the most difficult for us to accept as being even a small part of our human nature. However, this group is part of our soul cluster, and there is, even in the best and nicest of us, the capability for a little meanness, for ill will toward others, even of ungodly thoughts. But for most of us in the other four groups, this influence is most definitely uncharacteristic and will not come nearly as easily and naturally.

Whichever group is yours, whichever elemental energy source you are created from, this is the force that had primary influence on you prior to your life here on earth, this is the force that primarily influences you during your human existence, and this is the force that will primarily drive you forward on your soul's journey as you leave this earth and go out into the universe. This you cannot change.

We are all subject to, and have been influenced by, learned behavior. Our parents, our siblings, our peers, and others who have perhaps inspired us one way or another, along with our various worldly experiences and interactions, have sometimes taught us to control or suppress certain of our natural emotions and actions.

A Fire sign, extremely strong willed, not normally passive at all, may well, through many difficult emotional trials, have learned to hold back, to keep their emotions in check, having learned the error of always reacting through emotions. Even so, they will find this learned behavior a struggle to maintain and will always have to work at it.

An Earth sign, a powerfully strategizing soul, may have become, through learned behavior, a somewhat pushy and demanding individual. Undoubtedly recognizing this behavior as negative, they will dislike themselves for it.

An Air sign, naturally passive and easygoing, may well have learned to speak up for what they want, but perhaps in an aggressive and inappropriate manner. Not an instinctive thing for them to do, but learned behavior stemming from frustration and a feeling of being oppressed.

A Water sign, a compromising and evaluating soul, may have struggled in a relationship where compromise meant becoming a doormat and become assertive and uncompromising in what they feel are important issues, even though they may not like themselves as much.

Interestingly, if we look at families where there are a number of children, all nurtured in the same environment, influenced by the same people, going to the same schools, we see that each child responds in different ways, has different coping methods. Have you wondered why your brother seemed to love your sister more than you? Why your father seemed always at loggerheads with your brother? Why you and your grandmother had that special relationship? Why your parents always argued, or rarely did? Energy. It's all about the types of energy that were pervasive in your environment.

We can learn to harness that energy. The more we learn about our own energy group and the others, the more control we can gain over our lives and the environment in which we live. We can use this knowledge of energy constructively; to mature. Maturity allows for expansion, growth, openness, developing ourselves to the fullest. When we suppress our true selves, we do the opposite. We stunt our growth, we close off, we become less than we are. We do not mature. So we need to take all of those wonderful traits we have and expand them, show them off. Those traits that are not so wonderful will begin to change and improve as we expand what is good about ourselves. We have to learn, to dare to be all that we are, not less. We should strive to become rich and full with the promise of fulfillment. That's what maturity is.

There are Fire signs who as children had outbursts and temper tantrums but who have found a more mature way of thinking, a better way to express themselves. They still have those same feelings and urges, but now they use their energy positively, and therefore more powerfully. There are also those Fire signs who have learned nothing, who don't want to learn, who are content to reek havoc on themselves and others.

There are Earth signs who have learned not to try and control everyone and everything in every situation. Grown and matured, they realize that all they should really control is themselves. This doesn't come easily, given their particular driving energy force, and they still have that tendency to control, but maturity helps. Maturity is about expanding your horizons, learning to express yourself in a positive way. Maturity means daring to be your best self. Learning through experience how to use your energy positively brings fulfillment, a far richer life, and less conflict.

Air signs who have been suppressed in childhood can become angry and prone to use their energy in a negative way, becoming passive-aggressive, causing misunderstandings, bad communication, and confusion for themselves and others. They may have learned to expose the most aggressive side of their nature as a result of being exposed to bad parenting or aggressive siblings. Many, though, have learned to use their energy maturely, and can speak up and say how they feel in an appropriate manner and at an appropriate moment.

Some Water signs have learned that it isn't good for them always to evaluate a problem away, that they should act when action is appropriate and that there is a reasonable limit to compromise. There are, of course, those who cannot or rather will not grow, but it will be to their own detriment and that of those around them.

Sulphur signs have also come to this earth to learn, to grow, to mature. And just like the rest of us, through learned behavior, will either succeed or not. Finding ways, often through the examples of their upbringing, to use their own particular driving energy force in ways that enhance their abilities, they will affect their own lives and will most definitely affect the lives of those around them—always adversely.

All of us, even Sulphur signs in their evil intent, have the opportunity to become better or worse, more or less positive, more or less expressive. We must look beyond how we learned to be, to see what areas of behavior we might struggle with, what instinctive nature we sometimes feel we have to battle. As adults we learn to control or mask our natural, our instinctive energy. To find our soul group and ourselves, we need to look at what comes naturally, at what our natural and instinctive inclinations and reactions are.

We are all of us flowers in a garden rich with the nutrients we need to blossom. What choices will you make? What kind of bloom do you want to be? For me, there is only one choice: to be the best that I can be.

Interacting throughout our lives with those who surround us, and involved as we are in our own lives and in the lives of others, all of our experiences, good and bad, are nourishment for the soul.

As we have learned, much of the soul's nourishment comes from the type of energy we surround ourselves with each day from the people in our environment, and so it's important to be with people and in situations compatible with our own particular energy force. For most of us, particularly in the workplace, this isn't always possible, and we all have to learn to compromise—harder for some than for others, as we have seen. With our friends it is easier. We get to choose them. In our social lives it is also easier. If you go to a party, a dinner, a wedding, or some other social function and feel tension, friction, or angst, you can leave. Families, though, are an entirely other issue, and often can be a real problem. Clashes of energy inevitably occur when a mix of incompatible souls are forced together.

For example, let's say a boss who is usually easygoing and generally passive (an Air sign) turns on you and bites your head off for no good reason.

His behavior . . . uncharacteristic? Well, the bosses above him are giving him a hard time. The pressure is on. Frustrated and feeling oppressed, he snaps, but only for a moment. Driven by his natural energy force, to act only through frustration, he simply couldn't help it.

Or, your mostly caring, concerned, and loving mother is helping you plan your wedding. But suddenly it isn't your wedding anymore! The planning has gone to her head. She strategizes about your big day, forgetting to ask your opinions (she's an Earth sign). She strives to create the best and most impressive show. Driven by her natural energy force, she makes her lists and plans and then takes action. She takes initiative. She just can't help it. (As an Earth sign with a daughter, I really relate to this and am trying to pay attention.)

Consider a child who, strong-minded and strong willed, is prone to tantrums, either quietly or loudly defiant of anyone who tries to make him do what he doesn't want to do. He easily bursts into tears or rages, needing to express himself. Driven by his willful and somewhat uncompromising energy force (Fire, of course), he wants everything to be all about him and will take most things to heart, which can be difficult for the rest of the family to appreciate. The child, unfortunately, can't help it.

Or take a nurse who is left in charge of his patients for a few hours, with strict instructions from his supervisor to go by the rules. Normally he has no problem with that, as he reasons and evaluates that without rules, chaos would erupt. However, one of his patients, a young woman dying of cancer, a Fire sign, driven by emotion to break as many rules as she can and realizing she has very little time left to abide by or break any rules at all, wants to go out onto the patio and sit for a while in the sun. The nurse knows it's against doctor's orders to let the patient out of bed. He also knows that the patient has only a short time to live. What will he do? A Fire sign would be driven to do just what they felt at the moment, take the patient out onto the patio and ignore the rules and regulations. An Earth sign may well have made the same choice, but would strategize, if only briefly, making quite sure they wouldn't get caught, then would take the patient out onto the patio. An Air sign would be inclined to be more responsible and would wait to ask the opinion of someone in a more senior position, unless the patient was bullying enough, in which case they might be talked into it but would feel either nervous or guilty. Driven by his need to compromise, our nurse, a Water sign, evaluates the situation and decides to keep the patient in her bed, obeying doctor's orders, but he wheels the bed into the patch of sunlight in front of the window, where his patient can look out onto the patio. He has to find that compromise. He simply can't help it. He's a Water sign.

In all relationships it is our natural energy, our driving force, that matters, that combines and unites or clashes. Understanding what energy force drives you, and which sources of energy you are compatible with, means having a real chance of success in all areas of your life.

We came to this world prepared, powered, supercharged with our own internal supply of fuel. This is what we call our life's breath, our life force. Some call it karma.

Each of us is able to use our power in a variety of different ways, and by combining our energy with that external and universal energy, God energy, we can become an even greater source of power. Most of us do this on a very conscious level. We use the power of prayer, the power of the belief in a greater power; some of us use the power of our lucky number, a rabbit's foot

AT WORK, REST, AND PLAY—
AND IN LOVE

Most of you have already decided, from what you have read so far, which energy group you belong to. Others may not yet have made a definite determination. "Can I be in more than one group?" you might ask. "Is it possible to be both Earth and Water, or Fire and Air?" The answer is no, absolutely not.

What can and does confuse us is that each of the four soul types is capable of feeling and dealing with situations in the same way, and getting the same results. What makes us different, what puts us firmly into the different categories of Fire, Earth, Air, Water, and Sulphur, is our life force, the elemental influence which propels us into action. It is not the end result of our actions that we need to look at, it is more the process: *how* we think, *how* we feel, what it is that goes on in our minds, our hearts. What influence is it, what type of energy is it that we instinctively feel? What type of energy is it that drives us to evaluate, to become frustrated, to be influenced by our emotions, or to strategize and then to act or not to act in one way or another?

In our work arena, in our leisure time, as we play, and in our romantic relationships, our particular energy group influences our emotions and actions. So here are some more real-life examples of the typical responses of our soul groups. Let's see how we'd react.

At work, one of your bosses continually plays favorites, and plays mind games with the staff. He or she promotes and shows favor without discretion.

Would you

- Lash out in anger?

- Fume and feel bitter about the situation and complain to others?

- Feel personally victimized or hurt?

- Watch and wait for the opportunity to strike and have your way?

Any or all of these would be typical responses of a **Fire** sign.

Or would you

- Feel the injustice of the situation and make a plan to change the environment in which you work, which might involve going to a higher authority?

- Speak privately with the boss about the unfairness of the situation?

- Organize with your fellow workers a protest of some kind?

- Plan to look for another job?

Any or all of these would be typical responses of an **Earth** sign.

Or would you

- Accept that you have no real say in the matter?

- Try not to get involved and stay out of the way, feeling that it is really not your place to say or do anything?

- Make the best of a bad situation and hope that it will change at some point?

- Shrug it off and simply move on?

Any or all of these would be typical responses of an **Air** sign.

Or would you

- Try to evaluate why your boss would behave in such a way and work out what effect his behavior is having on you and your coworkers?

- Evaluate the importance of any input you might have as to whether you personally could alter the situation, and from your deductions and evaluations speak out?

- Say and do nothing?

- Give the benefit of right intention to your boss and try to keep the peace between him and your fellow workers?

Any or all of these would be typical responses of a **Water** sign.

At home, your spouse has invited a whole group of people to dinner without asking you. Some of the group are people you know and some are friends or work colleagues of your partner. You've had a tough day and had intended to relax, put your feet up, eat takeout, and watch television.
Would you

- Invite them in, order takeout, have a good time, and, after everyone is gone, kill your partner?

- Explode in anger and storm off to bed?

- Make the best of it but stew for a few days and make your partner suffer?

- Be thrilled and enjoy yourself?

Any or all of these would be typical responses of a **Fire** sign.

Or would you

- Accept the situation, feed everyone, and exit to the bedroom as soon as you can without spoiling the evening?
- Do what you had planned to do and let your spouse get on with their own plan, feeling no guilt at leaving them to their own devices?
- Enjoy the spontaneity of the evening and strategize with your partner so that you can all have a good time?
- Make a plan to speak to your partner later about that little phone call they should have made on the way home?

Any or all of these would be typical responses of an **Earth** sign.

Or would you

- Feel resentful of your partner's inconsiderate behavior toward you but make the best of it?
- Accept the situation and either enjoy it or simply keep your distance?
- Keep your feelings to yourself, even though you feel shy and a little awkward at being placed in the situation?
- Sneak off to bed when you can and hope that nobody notices?

Any or all of these would be typical responses of an **Air** sign.

Or would you

- Compromise with your partner, order takeout, eat, and then go watch TV and be happy that everyone else is having a good time?

- Be thoroughly annoyed with your partner but try to understand their reasons?

- Make the best of the situation and try to reason with your spouse later about the inconsiderate action?

- Try to come to an understanding with your spouse about future behavior?

Any or all of these would be typical responses of a **Water** sign.

You have been invited to a function; it might be a wedding, a fancy business dinner, the theater, or maybe an important family get-together. You really don't want to go but have been made to feel obligated, to feel guilt if you do not go—emotional blackmail.

Would you

- Feel furious at yourself for feeling guilty and refuse to go?

- Go, but make your feelings known and leave as quickly as you can?

- Try to change the venue or call others and influence them to do things *your* way?

Any or all of these would be typical responses of a **Fire** sign.

Or would you

- Quietly make other arrangements and feel little or no guilt?
- Go, but take someone with you whom you know you can have fun with?
- Evaluate your actions against the feelings of others and go, making the best of it, or not go, with no feelings of guilt?

Any or all of these would be typical responses of an **Earth** sign.

Or would you

- Accept the situation and simply live through it?
- Feel frustrated and upset at having to go, maybe show some emotion to those close to you but say nothing to those responsible?
- Keep your feelings of frustration to yourself and pretend you have another engagement but have pangs of guilt?

Any or all of these would be typical reactions of an **Air** sign.

Or would you

- Make up your mind to go, try to keep the peace, and do what you can to ensure that everyone you know has a good time despite the circumstances?

- Go for part of the time or arrange another time when you can all get together?

- Think up a way to have a good time?

Any or all of these would be typical responses of a **Water** sign.

As you can see by these examples, some of the feelings, emotions, and actions taken in each of the groups seem to be similar, with similar results. We make the best of things, we do or don't go to a party, we find ourselves another job; but how we arrive at those decisions, the process we go through, our *driving force*, our feelings—these are the internal forces that help us determine our energy type.

Are we driven by our emotions, our feelings of joy or passion, anger or hurt, trying to control and sometimes out of control ourselves, as our Fire signs are? *Reacting*.

Are we driven by a conscious and deliberate suppression, a laying aside of our emotions, replaced by a need to plan and strategize, as our Earth signs do? *Proactive*.

Are we driven to act only through frustration or oppression, being generally easygoing and happy, mostly following the flow of others, as our Air signs do? *Nonactive*.

Are we driven by our need to be reasonable, to live and let live, to keep the peace, to evaluate, as our Water signs do? *Interacting*.

All of us are capable of all of the feelings and emotions, the actions and reactions, the responses, of all of the rest of us. It is how we internalize our feelings and emotions, how we use them, and what drives the actions and reactions we are most likely to have that places us in our respective categories.

Ultimately, we respond and react to our life experiences in ways that lead us to spiritual growth. Each of us with our own set of strengths and weaknesses. We all have traits that give us power, and we all have traits that can make us powerless.

In personal relationships we look for our most compatible partner, that person with whom we somehow instantly make a special connection. The one you imagine you will be able to give the most to and who will, in return, give the most to you. We all dream of a soul mate. What we are looking for is a combination of energies that will not easily clash, that will knit together perfectly with our own energy. Finding your soul mate doesn't mean you live argument free for the rest of your lives, as each soul's character traits play a large part in determining how much peace and fulfillment there will be. But being with someone in a compatible energy group ensures that your relationship has a better chance of success.

Where one might be angry and upset, the influence of energy from the other will be appropriately calming and reasonable.

Where one might be nervous or afraid, the other would be strong and reassuring.

Where one might be easily irritated, the other would flow with the appropriate energy to deal most effectively with their moody mate.

Is it possible to find our soul mate? Of course it is. But it is easier for some soul signs than it is for others.

Fire signs, emotionally driven, will plow ahead if the mood takes them but will quickly move on to someone else if things don't go their way. Very tough if you're in a relationship with an Earth sign who is set on his course.

Earth signs, as the planners, the strategists, and the doers, have a natural inclination toward being constructive but can sometimes be too extreme, too demanding of themselves and others. This is hard on relationships.

Air signs, as the easygoing soul group, will have to feel that something is really important before they commit. They can often be swayed by a more determined and dogged soul sign, which sounds like it might make for a balanced relationship—unless or until our Air sign begins to feel unfulfilled or put upon.

Water signs go with the flow, which means that they are inclined to be committed to a relationship when it works, and to stray from that commitment when it doesn't work so well. Because they are a flowing and usually steady stream of energy, they are easy to be around, and this can be really good in relationships, particularly with Fire signs and Earth signs.

So from which energy source is your soul mate likely to come?

On the surface, especially if your idea of a good relationship is a peaceful and harmonious one, the relationships which seem most balanced are those between Air signs and Water signs—one partner being fairly passive and easygoing, the other partner always ready to compromise, equals less of an inclination to clash. And even when these two souls do clash—and of course they do—both partners are more than willing to find common ground and a way to work things out that benefits them both. This doesn't necessarily mean they have a perfect marriage or relationship; it means only that the flow of energy between Air signs and Water signs is very compatible, therefore the chance for a successful match is higher than between other signs.

Now, I can hear all of you Fire and Earth signs groaning in despair, just as I did. Remember, my child and I are Earth signs too, so does that mean our search for happiness is fruitless? No, it does not, not at all, although it does mean that we have to take a little more care when choosing the partner we hope to spend the rest of our lives with.

Finally, we have the key. We don't have to take unnecessary chances—we have a means to really figure out our love life and find true happiness. We don't have to make the same mistakes over and over again. Our sons and daughters don't have to make hard choices or wonder what their chances of divorce or loneliness will be. The game of love is no longer hit-or-miss, a shot in the dark. No longer is love a game of chance.

Life is a juggling act, relationships take work, and however we do it, no matter how successfully, one way or another, most of us manage a reasonable balance in our lives. We make up for the imbalance of our personal relationships by putting our various energies into other areas. We may plow our energies into our work and find compatible people to be around who make us feel good. We may find like souls whom we can relate to and share our lives with, who fulfill our needs as we fulfill theirs.

PART · THREE

SOUL SIGNS

   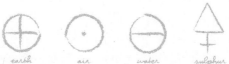

fire   earth   air   water   sulphur

A HOST OF GOLDEN DAFFODILS

Many years ago, when my child was young and I had lots of time, I was a gardener. I spent long hours planning and creating the best garden I could. Known especially for my roses, my garden was full of flowers. I particularly loved seeing the different varieties of daffodils first thing in the spring. As the years have gone by I have had less and less time to be a gardener, and rarely do I plant or grow anything these days. Then came the miracle of soul signs, and so here I am, a gardener again, but this time I am a gardener of souls.

In our garden of souls, each soul sign emits its own distinct kind of energy, produces its own special light, its own special bloom. Just as the different varieties of narcissus or daffodil bulbs produce unique flowers, so the thirteen soul signs in God's garden, in our soul cluster, do the same. Thirteen soul signs, all of us blowing in a breeze of uncertainty—excitement, fear, trepidation, happiness, laughter, tears, pain—all of those emotions that make up our lives. Soon we will go into great detail about each of the soul signs, so you can figure out which one you are. First, though, I'd like to share how the concept of soul signs came to me, and how each kind of soul is like a specific variety of daffodil.

I have been sitting in the sun, listening to the sound of far-off wind chimes, my pen poised above paper, waiting for inspiration, looking to Grey Eagle for guidance, when slowly I feel myself shifting into that twilight zone, that place where I glimpse the truth.

Where will I go this time, and what will I learn? Grey Eagle reaches for me, my gaze shifts, and I am vaguely aware that I am beginning to move. Down, down, down, I am definitely moving faster now, flowing from the physical world through the barrier that separates us from the place where all is known, a place familiar to me. On I go, down, down, into that familiar "other world" where all my senses are in tune.

First I see a large white flower, maybe a magnolia, its scent powerful yet not overpowering. Beyond that I see hills, rolling hills of the most luscious green, with grassy banks where sheep, just a few, seem to be grazing. Looking around, I catch a glimpse of red flowers, a stream, and a small rounded bridge made of stone. As I look more closely, I see that the bridge seems almost suspended above ground level. There are people walking on the grassy banks, and like the bridge they too seem slightly suspended, as if walking on air. All are barefoot yet clothed, and a breeze, though I cannot feel it, is picking up the folds of the ladies' dresses and playing a tune through their hair. Time, like the bridge and the people, seems suspended, and at this moment I hear no sound. It seems as if I am watching a silent movie that's unfolding in slow motion.

Quite suddenly a huge moon appears, filling the center of my field of vision. It does not seem dark, yet nor is it daylight, not yet. Swans, eagles, and many other birds are near.

I lift my head and, still smelling the scent of the white flower, now there is another smell, wonderful and sweet. My mind struggles for recognition and this I know: I am in Heaven, or at least a part of it.

I hear laughter coming from behind me. Lots of giggling, the sounds of children. The first I see, a boy, has his head shaved. His eyes are large and brown and he gazes at me, his face free of emotion. A lump in my throat, I think I recognize the child, Mark, my first child patient, and I wonder, "Will he smile for me, or will his expression stay the same?" He half turns away from me, looking backward to a place I cannot see. Then, turning back, he smiles a little, and I am content that he is well.

Strange that it should matter, yet I cannot help my humanness, and I look to see what he is wearing: trousers, a tunic in creamy white tied in the middle with a dark cloth belt. It reminds me of the outfit I wore when I took Judo lessons many years ago, and silently I ask the question, "Is this some kind of uniform?" An almost imperceptible movement of his head tells me he has heard my question and the answer is no. Then, as if that didn't happen, for a moment longer he stands before me, his face impassive—and then he is gone. The only sound I have heard so far, the sound of children laughing, is gone too. I am left alone in a surreal stillness.

Then a hand, a child's hand, comes out of nowhere to take my own. I cannot see, not yet, the body that belongs to the small fingers, but I know for certain that I am meant to follow the child.

Slowly, slowly, I feel myself lifted, still holding the tiny hand of the child who will be my guide. We float freely together, and my soul stirs somewhere within me.

The journey seems to take a while and yet no time at all. I know immediately when we arrive at our destination. There are fields and fields of golden blooms blowing in the breeze, more than I can begin to count, and I know that in some strange and inexplicable way, I can see with spirit eyes all the humanness of the world. I wonder for a moment if I am right, and I feel an instant confirmation as the child squeezes my hand.

As I gaze in wonderment and awe at the beauty of it, at the beauty of us, our human soul cluster, the words of William Wordsworth's poem "I Wandered Lonely as a Cloud" come into my mind.

I wandered lonely as a cloud

That floats on high o'er vales and hills,

When all at once I saw a crowd,

A host, of golden daffodils.

Now I hear sound again, as many children's voices fill the air. A tug on my hand breaks my reverie, and I begin to pay attention, for I know I have been brought here for a reason and I must learn as much as I can.

I look again at the fields of daffodils and see more movement: children playing among the flowers, children who will be, for this moment, my teachers. "Pay attention, pay attention, pay attention," they say. "Soul signs . . ."

"A garden of souls," I hear Grey Eagle whisper, "and there are twelve in all. Twelve of God, twelve of God, twelve of God."

I watch, and I listen, and the children begin to sing, and as they sing I notice they have formed four groups. Each group, moving in rhythm, dancing almost, weaving among the daffodils, each child chanting and singing a strange, strange song.

> *"This is for the Bright Star,*
>
> *Short-cupped and bright.*
>
> *This is for the Dreaming,*
>
> *Poeticus in the light.*
>
> *And this one for the Retrospective,*
>
> *Cyclamineus to help them see.*
>
> *And all in one big garden,*
>
> *And all of them with me.*

> *"This is for the Warrior,*
>
> *A Trumpet strong and brave.*
>
> *And this is for the Visionary,*
>
> *A Double that God gave.*
>
> *And this is for the Hunter,*
>
> *A Triandrus pure and white.*
>
> *And all in God's good garden,*
>
> *And all a wondrous sight.*

"So now we have the Newborn,

Split cupped and open wide.

And here we have the Prophet,

Tazetta blooms you cannot hide.

And then we have the Traveler,

Many-faceted, takes your breath away.

And all in that same garden,

And all are there to stay.

"This is for the Old one,

Long-cupped, with centers pink.

And this is for the Peacemaker,

Jonquilla's beauty makes them think.

And this is for the Seeker,

Bulbicodium, rare and wild.

And all in one rich garden,

Each one a special child."

And on and on, and round and round, the children sang and danced, in and around the field of gold, the music sweet in my ears. These voices soon joined with many more I could not see, and then I too began to sing the song, and in this way I began to learn the lesson.

Time? There was no time, but after what seemed like a long while I began again to move, floating gently and slowly back, the song ringing in my head, the words held in my heart.

And then I am back, sitting in the sun, with only the sound of far-off wind chimes and my pen poised above the paper. Looking back to my inspired journey, not yet able to get the song out of my head, and realizing how incredible this gift of soul recognition is, I head for my bookshelves. My shelves are crammed with a variety of gardening books, and I pull them down, eager to see what my soul's energy might look like, what they all look like, trying to match the flower to the soul type.

But I am getting ahead of myself, wanting to talk about soul signs before you even know what they are. First, we recall, come the soul groups, those five elemental energy sources from which all souls on earth are created. These we know all about: Fire, Earth, Air, Water, and Sulphur. What we are about to learn, what I learned from Grey Eagle, is that in four of these groups there are three distinct soul signs, and that each one might be someone we know.

THIRTEEN SOULS

By now you know which elemental force drives you. You know your primary energy source, which energy pocket you belong to. The next step is to determine your soul sign.

As we're all related blooms in this earthly garden of souls, we are alike in many ways. We often behave similarly and think the same way others do, so it will take some reflection on our part to identify the one sign that defines our soul, that explains us. But there are solid behavioral clues as well as more subtle clues that have to do with how energy flows among the different energy groups and the signs themselves, so follow my lead closely and you should have no problem accessing the knowledge Grey Eagle has passed on about your spiritual destiny.

There are thirteen soul signs altogether, each powered and influenced by one of the five energy groups.

In our **Fire** group we have

The Retrospective Soul

The Dreaming Soul

The Bright Star Soul

The Fire energy group of souls is driven by and acts through emotion.

In our **Earth** group we have

The Hunter Soul

The Visionary Soul

The Warrior Soul

The Earth energy group of souls is driven by and acts through planning and strategizing.

In our **Air** group we have

The Traveler Soul

The Prophet Soul

The Newborn Soul

The Air energy group of souls is driven by and acts through frustration and oppression.

In our **Water** group we have

    The Seeker Soul

    The Peacemaker Soul

    The Old Soul

The Water energy group of souls is driven by and acts through evaluation and compromise.

And in the **Sulphur** group we have

    The Dark Soul

The Sulphur energy group of souls is driven by and acts through a desire to corrupt.

As you can see in this first look at how our soul cluster is divided, there are four energy groups with three soul signs in each—"Twelve of God," says Grey Eagle. In our final group, Sulphur, we have one soul, the Dark Soul. (All three manifestations of the Dark Soul are created from the same elemental force, but each uses its dark energy in a different way; I'll elaborate on this in a future chapter.) Which specific soul sign are you? By looking at the list of signs attached to your energy group, above, you have already narrowed the field to three; you are definitely one of these.

Be careful not to assume immediately that the name of a specific soul sign implies a certain type of person or characteristic. It does not. For instance, you might assume that a Hunter Soul is a person who likes to go out into the woods and hunt deer and other animals. Not necessarily so. You might assume that a Newborn Soul is a person who behaves childishly. Again, not necessarily so. You also might think that someone who travels a lot is obviously a Traveler Soul. Don't assume. Don't allow the name to color your judgment as you try to figure out who you are.

Rather, let's take a close look together now at the primary character traits of each of our soul signs, along with an overview of how they relate to others and a glimpse at the uniqueness of their bloom.

As you read the descriptions that follow of the three soul signs in your energy group, use a process of elimination. One of the descriptions will definitely not be you; cast out that soul sign. Now you have only two choices. Don't expect that either description will be one hundred percent you. Remember, you will be reading the character traits of your soul, and through your upbringing, your environment, your learned behavior, some traits will be more obvious to you and some will be less so. Of your two choices, you are likely to say of one, "Yes, that could be me, that sounds a lot like me," but then you might say of the other, "Wait, *that's* me, that sounds much more like me." Or, if you really know yourself well, you might say immediately, "That is definitely me." In any case, do read each of the soul-sign descriptions carefully. Identifying which sign you are is the basis for figuring out exactly how your soul interacts with others in this earth realm.

Let's begin with the Fire signs: The Retrospective Soul, The Dreaming

Soul, and The Bright Star Soul. Our song tells us that their respective flowers are the Cyclamineus, the Poeticus, and the Short-cupped daffodil.

The Retrospective Soul

The Retrospective Soul is probably one of if not *the* most misunderstood of all the soul signs, mainly because of their real difficulty in seeing themselves as they really are, as they can be so blinded by and so trapped in their emotions. Extremely strong willed and emotionally driven, learning and growing is an extremely painful process for the Retrospective Soul. Misunderstood, and often unfairly and harshly judged by others, it takes a truly courageous Retrospective to open their eyes, to accept who they are and why they behave as they do, but when that happens, the flower that is their spirit shines through with blinding beauty.

My friend Jack is a great example of a Retrospective Soul. He is, without a doubt, one of the most hard-working and conscientious men I have ever known. Jack is also willing to help anyone, he is kind and generous with the biggest heart, and everyone who meets him has only the best things to say about him. You would think that because he is obviously so well respected and so well loved that he would be a really happy man. But no, there is always some problem, or a potential problem, always a negative. Jack just can't help it—he focuses time and time again on the negative. He struggles with past hurts and pain, he struggles with his own self-worth, and no matter how good his life is, it is never enough. But despite this, he is very special to me. His intentions are always the best, and I am so thankful that he and his wife are a big part of my life.

Willful and somewhat uncompromising, as all Fire signs are, the Retrospective soul has probably the most difficult life struggle of the thirteen soul types, which is easy to explain.

This soul truly and intensely desires perfection. They feel the need to want everything to be perfect: a perfect marriage, a perfect child, a perfect job, a perfect pet, a perfect life. But most of us know that life isn't like that. In the beginning of any relationship, the Retrospective Soul tends to look through rose-colored glasses, believing that this new person, this new situation, will be perfect. Inevitably, the Retrospective Soul will be disappointed again and again. They will feel let down and inadequate and will often blame others, unable or unwilling to see that perhaps their expectations were set too high.

Character Traits of the Retrospective Soul

Extremely idealistic, hardworking, a survivor; can be kind and considerate when seeking attention and approval, although this soul always has to struggle with feelings of insecurity. Takes things personally—a worrier. Tends to continually look back, holding on tightly to old hurts and pain, and may find it difficult to separate past and present. Is ultrasensitive and therefore easily hurt. Prone to disappointment and often finds it a struggle to be positive; can become self-involved and, because of focusing on negative past experiences, if not careful can become a malcontent.

In initial encounters, the Retrospective Soul will have high expectations, can have moments of great insight and sensitivity, but later can be seen by some as a cave dweller or ostrich, burying their head in the sand, often in denial, with a tendency to repeat past mistakes. Finds it difficult to express feelings except through emotionally driven outpourings. Might use health problems to excuse bad behavior.

Has two opposite sides: is caring, sympathetic, and warm in nature, and because of a great need to be needed will willingly put themselves out to help others, especially those outside the family who have not yet disappointed them; but within the family they tend to hold on to their disappointment, and in their need to be in control have been known to go as far as to create sibling rivalries as a means of controlling the family. Has particular difficulty with same-sex children, i.e., mother/daughter, father/son. If this soul doesn't mature, they have a tendency to grow more unhappy in old age.

RELATIONSHIPS AND THE RETROSPECTIVE SOUL

As a very needy person, strong willed and often willful, and unconsciously always looking for perfection, an idealist, the Retrospective Soul might find great difficulty in achieving any sense of personal happiness. Perhaps needs someone who will see through rose-colored glasses to the good inside. In maturity, though, the Retrospective Soul can be one of the most powerful and alluring of our soul cluster. Overcoming their disappointments and understanding their true nature, they will work doubly hard at making their relationships work, and will achieve that happiness they so desperately need and deserve.

DANGERS: Blaming others for things that go wrong; in denial of their own culpability; needing perfection, and therefore putting themselves and others in that impossible situation of continual disappointment.

Song of the Retrospective Soul

The Retrospective Soul, a Fire sign, is matched to the Cyclamineus. "To help them see," says the song, and as I study the Cyclamineus more closely, I do see. If any picture could tell a story, this would be it. Having a windswept appearance, the flower hangs down—the struggle of the Retrospective is made apparent. Yet there is something fine and rare and beautiful about these deep yellow blooms that speaks of the Retrospective Soul's potential in maturity.

The Dreaming Soul

You cannot help but like the Dreaming Soul, as they have so many endearing qualities. Even at the height of frustration with their scatterbrained antics, it is hard to hold on to any feelings of anger toward them, as their intentions are usually the best. If you have a Dreaming Soul in your life, then your life is enriched.

With their thoughts often going in several different directions at once, the Dreaming Soul will need to work on self-discipline—hard for them to do, but if they are willing to grow they can definitely achieve this, especially if they have a really specific goal. As a Fire sign they are extremely strong willed, but quietly so; their Fire, their passion, is well hidden.

The Dreaming Soul is driven to action through the emotions, as are all

Fire signs. However, their willfulness and their frequent refusal to compromise are much less obvious than with the other soul signs in their group. The Dreaming Soul is often underestimated for just that reason. As it does with all Fire signs, the phrase "You can take a horse to water, but you can't make it drink" comes to mind.

Character Traits of the Dreaming Soul

Aspires to wonderful things, ambitious but not driven, idealistic but not always living in what some would call the real world. Has a vivid imagination and a tendency to get carried away; is contemplative and often in their own head; not particularly physically active or prone to strenuous exercise, but walking, yoga, or similar, gentle mind-body exercises will interest them. The Dreaming Soul can be meditative, prone to wishful thinking, always expectant, and hopeful of life and situations; likes to avoid conflict but will fight when emotionally driven.

A Dreaming Soul can be thoughtful but also unsure of themselves, defensive. Happy to fantasize, with a quick sense of humor; artistic, creative, loves to paint or sew or be actively creative. Loves people, children, and animals. Very caring and desiring the best for others, they are willing workers and like to be helpful, but do not like to be in a position of authority and can easily get flustered.

Relationships and the Dreaming Soul

The Dreaming Soul is forgiving and tolerant, and often determined to see their mate through rose-colored glasses. Two Dreaming Souls can spell disaster, though, as a relationship generally needs at least one partner to be more realistic. This soul can allow herself to be taken advantage of, but only if she wants it that way; rarely dissatisfied and always hopeful of improvement, looking for a knight in shining amour with whom to live the fairy-tale marriage.

DANGERS: Being unrealistic and disappointed in their partner if the rose-colored glasses come off; not always seeing things as they really are; assuming that everyone else thinks the way they do.

SONG OF THE DREAMING SOUL

The Dreaming Soul is represented by the Poet-icus, a perfect match it seems. I smile as I remember the children singing, "Poeticus in the light," and surely when we see the bloom we can see that it is. One will only have to look at this bloom to see the connection to its soul sign.

The Bright Star Soul

Two of my closest friends are Bright Star Souls, and my life has been made so much more pleasurable—and difficult—by having them around. Wonderful and bright, they do indeed bring light and fun and laughter with them. The Bright Star seeks and needs attention in great quantities, and this is for most of us not always possible to give. The Bright Star can become emotional and easily hurt by what appears to them neglectful behavior by others. Ego is perhaps the Bright Star's Achilles heel, as their need to be number one can overshadow personal confidence, although that same ego, used positively, is what pushes them forward and helps them achieve. If not careful, the Bright Star's lack of introspection can halt or slow their growth, which will cause some difficulties.

As a Fire sign, the Bright Star is driven by emotion. Willful and somewhat uncompromising, as all Fire signs are, the Bright Star can be seen to be quite dramatic and a real powerhouse of energy.

CHARACTER TRAITS OF THE BRIGHT STAR SOUL

Talented, cheerful, quick-witted, and clever but often naive, quick to recover from difficult situations, alert, extremely optimistic, radiant, intelligent. Very principled but vivacious and usually lucky, the Bright Star Soul has a divine quality or a uniqueness that can be hard to define. A prominent performer in any chosen profession, often well known—even famous—and brilliant, many Bright Stars, especially in immaturity, like to be number one, even in the most insignificant events. Can have tendencies toward astronomy, astrology, or matters pertaining to planetary action.

Often attractive or handsome, even beautiful, and extremely headstrong and willful, Bright Stars can be dramatic to the point of being disregarded by others as attention seekers. They put great store in and value reputation in themselves and others.

Bright Star Souls have a tendency to orbit, to go around problems in order to solve them, and often do not get to the point quickly, with a tendency to procrastinate. An entertainer, a good host, usually has a good sense of humor, egotistical, needs to be liked or loved, and needs to feel appreciated and special. Usually has difficulty with introspection, and will often be confused by their own actions. Is easily hurt emotionally and tends to take everything personally.

RELATIONSHIPS AND THE BRIGHT STAR SOUL

Needs a partner who is quietly self-assured and confident, who will not mind taking a backseat and will not feel threatened by their mate's strong personality. Is a passionate lover, but for all that apparent boldness will take a while to warm up. Easily impressed and likes to be surrounded by beautiful and intelligent people, but will often mistake intelligence for sincerity and caring. Driven by emotion, the Bright Star can have incredible mood swings, and the emotional highs and lows will keep their partner on his or her toes—which can be exhausting but also exciting and fun.

DANGERS: Being too controlling and too dramatic to be taken seriously; demanding and somewhat needy, sometimes to the point of being blind to others' needs; wanting things their way.

SONG OF THE BRIGHT STAR SOUL

The Bright Star, a Fire sign, is matched to the Short-cupped daffodil. The shape alone determines this match. The flower's single bloom, star-shaped and golden yellow, its center red and beautifully bright with only one flower to a stem, cries out for attention, just as the Bright Star does.

Now we come to our Earth signs: The Hunter Soul, The Visionary Soul, and The Warrior Soul. Our song tells us that their flowers are the Triandrus, the Double daffodil, and the Trumpet daffodil.

⊕ The Hunter Soul

The Hunter can be a challenging and truly inspiring personality, actively working to achieve whatever it is they desire. In their determination to win, however, sometimes they can be unintentionally draining, damaging, and harmful to those around them. As with most soul types, their character traits can be equally negative or positive, and either way they are one of the strongest souls in our cluster, maximizing not only their own talents but also, to a lesser degree, the talents of others.

From the energy group of Earth, the Hunter is driven to action by a need to act, to plan, to strategize. When the Hunter uses that energy force negatively, we have one of the most difficult and aggressive soul signs. When that same force is used positively, we have one of the most productive of our soul signs—creative, energetic, and extremely powerful.

CHARACTER TRAITS OF THE HUNTER SOUL

Pursues goals, takes action, is skillful, artful, patient for their own needs. Exploitive of people and situations, or opportunistic? Prone to suppressing anger, and then has flare-ups. Might struggle in personal relationships and does not share easily. Likes own-sex company, likes physical activity, likes to be active and is often sports oriented; is an outdoors person and usually likes animals, as they can often relate better to them than to people. Is a tracker, keeps track of people and situations.

When it's important to them, the Hunter Soul can be a good provider, thinker, and planner, driving and ambitious, but can also be extremely self-motivated, self-propelled, pushy, and demanding. Has strong instincts, is a predator, unconsciously seeking out and using other souls' energies for themselves. Needy, wanting, forward, can be extremely selfish without realizing it; can be a know-it-all, proud, often seen by others as arrogant, very much a loner despite hating solitude, self-interested, can be quick and cunning. Has an explosive personality, is not always good-humored but has a good sense of humor, can become frustrated very easily. Has two sides: is controlling, likes to control people and situations; can be incredibly and surprisingly kind, but constantly seeks appreciation for even the smallest good deed—has a need to be recognized.

RELATIONSHIPS AND THE HUNTER SOUL

In the beginning of any relationship, the Hunter Soul works hard to be all that their good side is: charming, gentle, interested, and thoughtful. But they may have difficulty and will inevitably struggle to sustain this, and will need constant reminders that others' needs are important too. It will not take too long for their other side, their self-involved side, to show through. Needs someone with a strong but more passive nature who will be prepared to encourage and admire them, feeding their ego.

DANGERS: Ignoring others' needs and not easily learning to share, the Hunter is a soul very much into their own self and own needs, often (and most definitely unintentionally) at the expense of others, yet capable of seriously campaigning for others' rights, as long as their own personal interest is fired.

SONG OF THE HUNTER SOUL

The Hunter Soul, an Earth sign, is matched to the Triandrus daffodil. In our song, the children refer to this flower as "pure and white," which speaks of this soul's good intentions. As I look at the flower, its head hung down, I am reminded of the struggle of the Hunter Soul to look within. And yet, a truly  beautiful flower, it shows the Hunter's potential, and reminds us that the Hunter Soul is one of the strongest and most determined of our soul cluster.

⊕

The Visionary Soul

A Visionary Soul will make the best friend. Loyal and concerned, they rarely give up on anyone, and will take the initiative and call you, even if you neglect them. Because of this they are open to being used and can become extremely hurt by others' seeming insensitivity or neglect. However, they are very forgiving and rarely, if ever, hold a grudge. I am fortunate to be so blessed as to have a Visionary Soul for a daughter.

The Visionary is driven to action through planning, strategizing, and the need to act, as all Earth signs are; however, this characteristic is not as obvious in the Visionary as with the other souls in this group, although they are equally strong.

CHARACTER TRAITS OF THE VISIONARY SOUL

Good instincts, not easily trusting of others and their instincts, intuitive, understanding, sympathetic, empathetic, makes a good healer. Connected to things spiritual, connected to their soul, curious, in an unconscious state of awareness, wise, bright, able to reason and to be reasonable. Has great vision and is very insightful, and will often be profound in a way that can surprise even them. Very perceptive, a good judge of character, though not always practical and has the tendency to daydream. Has a remarkable imagination, can be unrealistic, has a tendency to procrastinate over difficult situations but will eventually make decisions and take action when necessary.

The Visionary Soul is a thinker, very moral, has an inquiring mind and a great amount of common sense but doesn't always apply it to themselves. A planner, is speculative, questioning. Can tend toward being negative about their own life situation and can on occasion become easily depressed, but at the same time is always hopeful, is prone to flights of fancy, and does not always keep their feet on the ground. With family, friends, and colleagues they will be protective. A Visionary will shine in their ability to sense others' emotional and spiritual states of mind, and to give really constructive advice, which they will not always take for themselves. A Visionary is insightful and has the ability to judge most situations with great perspective. Is not always good with money or material growth, and may well struggle financially.

RELATIONSHIPS AND THE VISIONARY SOUL

A Visionary needs practicality and a partner who has their feet on the ground. Needs to be protected and can often feel vulnerable in uncharted waters. Hates to be controlled, is very tactile and affectionate, but is easily mistrusting. A good homemaker, using planning and strategy to create a perfect environment.

DANGERS: May allow a strong partner to override their instincts; often not practical with money, and has a tendency to overspend; tends to need constant reassurance emotionally, which can strain a partnership.

SONG OF THE VISIONARY SOUL

The Visionary Soul, an Earth sign, is matched to the Double daffodil. The incredible beauty of this bloom takes my breath away, and I am at once both grateful and in awe as I am reminded of the potential of my own child's soul. Having one or more flowers to a stem and a clustered cup, this bloom shows the endless and timeless nature of the Visionary Soul's growth possibilities.

The Warrior Soul

The Warrior personality generally stands out, and can be found by some to be intimidating. Often at the forefront of any action, strong and steady and utterly reliable, this is a good person to have by your side in a fight, as the Warrior will bring sound common sense to any situation, and will act when others are uncertain or afraid.

The Earth-group drive for planning, strategizing, and taking action is very obvious in the Warrior. As a Warrior Soul myself, I know firsthand how in immaturity the Warrior can be forceful and judgmental in their demands of others, particularly when it comes to their idea of right behavior. In maturity the Warrior learns that they can control only their own behavior, and it is not for them to decide what is right or wrong for others—a tough lesson, but one well worth learning.

CHARACTER TRAITS OF THE WARRIOR SOUL

Combative, courageous, has many mental struggles, likes to strategize and so will often wrestle inwardly with problems before dealing with them. Doesn't give up, committed, brave, sees and watches like a hawk. Can be a hardliner. Is an expansionist, a crusader, very professional, can be mercenary for what they consider to be the greater good. Thoughtful, adventuresome, unafraid to do battle, a good planner. The first to volunteer for a good cause. A trooper, a campaigner, likes order, very hardworking, has great energy but not necessarily physical. Often has great faith in God and/or in themselves.

The Warrior Soul is precise, methodical, curious, meticulous, exacting, fastidious, regimented. Can be picky, rigorous, thorough, and painstaking, which can be challenging, although they are extremely protective of loved ones and the underdog. Infused with a sense of fairness and honesty, and when in battle is unafraid of personal harm. Has a strong sense of justice, hates meanness or injustice. Determined, aggressive when necessary, powerful, a good mediator. Outspoken, watchful, alert, quick-witted, and serious, even in humor. Concerned with self-growth. A true Warrior is not a fighter or a brawler but is very knowing.

RELATIONSHIPS AND THE WARRIOR SOUL

The Warrior Soul loves company and is usually very social. However, will tend to keep inner feelings private until a bond of trust has been formed. Is very much home oriented, so family is the priority. Personal relationships are important and built on trust. Needs a partner who is first loyal, centered, and sure of their own self—must understand and be protective of the Warrior's vulnerability.

DANGERS: Being too controlling and thinking they know best for others; being too rigid in their demands of right behavior.

SONG OF THE WARRIOR SOUL

The Warrior Soul is matched to the Trumpet daffodil: tall, strong, and proud. It stands as we might imagine a warrior would stand. The bloom of the bulb shows what, in maturity, is possible. The potential of the Warrior is amazing, and as we can see, the energy of the Trumpet flower is strong, bright, and delicate yet indestructible.

We continue now with our Air signs: The Traveler Soul, The Prophet Soul, and The Newborn Soul. Our song tells us that their flowers are the Many-faceted daffodil, the Tarzetta, and the Split corona.

The Traveler Soul

As I was married, it seems now like many lifetimes ago, to a Traveler Soul, I know firsthand how both the negatives and the positives of this soul sign work. The Traveler has great difficulty making personal commitments, and their fear that the grass may be greener on the other side of the fence can be taken to such an extreme that they can miss out on what is right under their nose, and fail to see or to take advantage of the moment. Age and experience can change this, and when that happens the Traveler can and will be less afraid to commit, and will be eager to act in a good and positive way. Work or career is important, and in these areas the Traveler will be much more decisive and committed, and will usually shine in their chosen career.

From the energy group of Air, the Traveler is driven to action through a need to express frustration or oppression, and is the most likely of the group to express that frustration—which is not necessarily a bad thing, particularly if that expression is nonaggressive; but as with all our Air signs, it will take a lot to see the aggressive side of the Traveler.

Character Traits of the Traveler Soul

An explorer, a good storyteller, is a dreamer and may be a true traveler and explorer of foreign lands. Has a tendency to ignore emotional issues, passively burying their head in the sand, hoping problems will simply go away. Is intuitive and often sensitive to psychic phenomena. Likes the movies, as movies take them to other dimensions, other places; often but not always very fond of books and poetry. Knowledgeable in certain chosen areas, can be inquisitive but does not necessarily have a good attention span, except in a working environment, unless they mean to impress. Would make a good salesperson.

The Traveler Soul is a romancer, can be very romantic but also fickle, especially in youth. Likes to be active, on the move. Is a thrill seeker; home comforts are not important except for some as a status symbol. Is a wanderer both physically and mentally. A good communicator, a nonconformist, interested in the world and world events more than in what is close at hand; eyes ever turned outward, rarely inward, a collector of facts, even trivial ones. Always on the lookout for the next new thing, rarely boring and has a good sense of humor, generally easygoing and accepting of others, passive but will blow up if they feel cornered or oppressed.

Relationships and the Traveler Soul

Likes falling in love, but when the first bloom falls, is ready to fall in love again with the next one. Is prone to marriage, as they are great romantics, but is the type to marry again and again or to have a variety of relationships. Likes family and kids but may initially shy away from responsibility and commitment. Needs an independent mate who will not mind their flirtatious nature. Will usually settle down in their mature years, mid to late forties or fifties, when they will be much more able to accept those responsibilities that they have, in the past, avoided.

DANGERS: Unintentional insensitivity to their partner's feelings; refusing to deal with emotional issues; thinking that the grass may be greener somewhere else when often it is not.

SONG OF THE TRAVELER SOUL

The Traveler Soul, an Air sign, is matched to the Many-faceted daffodil, which encompasses all those blooms that do not fit neatly into any of the other divisions. A mixture of delicate and perfect flowers speak for the soul of the Traveler. A nomad, somewhat of a nonconformist, extraordinary and special; our song says ". . . takes your breath away," and they surely do.

The Prophet Soul

The Prophet is perhaps the gentlest of the Soul cluster, with good intentions toward everyone. Has great faith in people, which can often lead to personal disappointment and unhappiness. Selfless to the point of self-damage, and passive in nature, a Prophet Soul will rarely show aggression—

but watch out when they do. The Prophet is one of those souls we need if we are sick or hurt, as they will work tirelessly for the good of others.

From the energy group of Air, the Prophet is driven to action only through frustration or oppression, and will, much more easily than the other two signs in that group, be able to deal with any feelings of aggression or frustration in a calmer and more balanced way, rarely allowing themselves to become embroiled in aggravating or argumentative situations, staying for the most part calm and centered.

CHARACTER TRAITS OF THE PROPHET SOUL

Has an inborn faith in God, an inner knowing and a real connection to their spirit self. Likes having a cause. Is a good interpreter, very sensitive, intuitive, caring, and gentle; concerned about others and the world much more than they are about themselves. Foresighted, with a quiet and even mysterious side; a good forecaster of other people's feelings. Makes a good healer, doctor, or nurse. Will have a tendency to seek work in the service of others, even if it is only on a part-time or voluntary basis. Loves animals and would make a good veterinarian, farmer, zookeeper, or animal caretaker.

The Prophet Soul seeks wisdom but is not necessarily wise; likes books that have a purpose or meaning or in some way are constructive and instructive. Can be quite opinionated. Very trusting and accepting of others, although can at times be passive to the point of allowing others to abuse their good nature. Truthful, honest, sometimes a little fanciful, a great thinker but not necessarily a doer. Can be somewhat naive in trusting. Loves children and often finds it easier to communicate with them than with adults. Can be a loner and is often lonely, outgoing but in a very quiet way, very family oriented, generally content with life and able to make the best of even the worst situations.

RELATIONSHIPS AND THE PROPHET SOUL

Family is most important to the Prophet Soul, who needs a partner that is also family oriented and a willing participant in the family or parenting process. Needs a partner who is perhaps a little more gregarious and outgoing, but not too much so.

DANGERS: Being drawn to the needy, or what we might term a troubled soul. For example, a Retrospective Soul would be drawn to the Prophet, but this would be a dangerous mix for both, as the Prophet would give to their own detriment, and the Retrospective, without meaning to, would take, also to their own detriment.

SONG OF THE PROPHET SOUL

The Prophet Soul, an Air sign, is matched to the Tazetta daffodil, and as the song says, these are "blooms you cannot hide." It makes my heart sing when I realize that there are such wonderful souls among our soul cluster. As I look at them, these blooms, these clusters  of pale yellow and deeper-yellow-centered flowers, and their incredible fragrance, speak of trust and honesty. And they show the Prophet soul as it truly is: incredibly centered and perhaps just a little fanciful.

The Newborn Soul

The Newborn Soul is one of my personal favorites. If you know someone who is this soul sign, you will know instantly what I mean. You can only think of that person with a smile on your face. The Newborn is a soul who is mostly tolerant and accepting of others, and will usually give everyone a chance. The Newborn is an obvious and very positive Air sign.

The Newborn is no pushover, however, and is perfectly capable of standing their ground when they have to. Still, a very likeable and generally easygoing type.

CHARACTER TRAITS OF THE NEWBORN SOUL

Naive, obvious, easy to read, easily influenced, inquisitive and inquiring of people, but in a really good way. Fresh, interested in most things, simple, finds it hard to keep a secret. Prone to gossip, but without any meanness or intention of doing harm. Inventive, curious, can be unintentionally insensitive. Seemingly immature in some ways, can be innovative, original, gimmicky. Likes to be up-to-date about things—artistic, inventive, and creative. Likes to be a trendsetter. Is sometimes slow to grasp situations but can be surprisingly constructive.

The Newborn Soul can be emotional, and is often hard to control. A nonconformist, is nontraditional, innocent, open, pliable; amateurish, youthful, bold; gentle, sensitive, likes people, loves nature, has very few dislikes. Has a tendency to be too trusting. Makes friends easily, and often has long-standing relationships with high school or college friends from twenty years ago or more. Likes to please, and will fit into most situations easily; likes to belong, and is also easy to please. Can be self-indulgent, especially with food or drink. Is capable of aggressive action, but only when really pushed.

RELATIONSHIPS AND THE NEWBORN SOUL

This soul is extremely easygoing, which may be a problem for some soul signs. Sometimes finds it hard to make decisions, especially important ones, and will often defer to a stronger partner. Is impulsive and falls in love easily, but is in the relationship for the long haul. Very loyal and affectionate, but can be found by some souls to be somewhat irritating without meaning to be, as they are often, in their naïveté, really enthusiastic over the smallest thing. Loves children and animals, both of which are important features for them in their ideal home life.

DANGERS: Not paying attention and getting carried away in their own activities; in their desire to like and to be liked by others, the Newborn Soul is apt to ignore their instincts and sometimes make misjudgments of other people's character.

SONG OF THE NEWBORN SOUL

The Newborn soul is matched to the Split corona, a splendid bloom. "Split cupped, and open wide," sang the children, and indeed it is. It is just the most perfect match for our Newborn soul—open, accepting, and welcoming. The colors of yellow and orange speak of the light and joy of its soul match, and as you look at the flower, you can see immediately how open and fresh the bloom is. Just like the soul of the Newborn.

Our fourth group contains our Water signs: The Seeker Soul, The Peacemaker Soul, and The Old Soul. The song tells us that their flowers are the Bulbocodium, the Jonquilla, and the Long-cupped daffodil.

The Seeker Soul

The Seeker can be a somewhat difficult person to get to know, as there is a lot going on inside that they find hard to share. This soul sign is wonderful to be around at a party, as they have a lot to say and are usually well informed.

From the energy group of Water, the Seeker is driven to action through a need to evaluate and compromise. The Seeker will usually do what they want, but will try to evaluate a situation around to their way of thinking and to find some kind of compromise with others. They may take, and be able to justify their actions, but will usually try to give something back in return.

Character Traits of the Seeker Soul

Inquiring, likes trying new things, is unafraid of asking questions or showing curiosity. Can often be uncertain but won't show it; can have problems with low self-esteem. Principled, self-controlled, can seem to be emotionless, dispassionate, or detached but is mostly coolheaded. Extremely introspective, can be inwardly critical of others. Rational, intuitive, conceptual, deducing and evaluating, argumentative, and aggressive when pushed. Mentally alert, can be idealistic, likes experimenting. Studious, loves a challenge. A good compromiser. Loves books and music, likes movies and the arts, likes companionship.

The Seeker can be quietly questioning of others while often not questioning of their own actions; can be self-righteous. Avaricious in their quest for knowledge, a collector of facts, even trivial ones. Sees themselves as philosophers and are philosophical in their thinking; would make a good teacher but would stay removed emotionally from students. Is often good at expressing and communicating knowledge but finds it hard to express personal feelings and emotions. Considers self intellectual and likes to mix with serious-minded and intelligent people. Usually knows many people and has lots of acquaintances but few close friends. In immaturity, the Seeker will have a tendency to use people and situations to their own advantage, sometimes without regard to another's feelings. Maturity can and does change this.

Relationships and the Seeker Soul

Personal involvements scare the Seeker, who will rarely make the first move. It takes a quietly determined soul type to pin them down, and their intellectual ego is the way to this one's heart. Once captured, the seeker will make a good wife/husband/provider and will take their role seriously.

DANGERS: Holding back, being somewhat aloof or reserved, withholding. Maturity can change this, but only with the greatest effort on their part.

SONG OF THE SEEKER SOUL

The Seeker Soul, a Water sign, is matched to the Bulbocodium, and like this flower, with its wild variants and hybrids, the Seeker, as our song says, "is rare and wild." The bloom shows the need of its soul match to be separate and apart from others, always seeking, different, yet still needing to be a part of the soul cluster, part of our garden of souls.

The Peacemaker Soul

If you have a friend you just want to shake because they are too good, too nice, and too often used by others, they may well be a Peacemaker. One of my students comes very much to mind as I am writing, as just a few days ago in my healing development class we had a lesson about selfishness, that it's okay to be selfish sometimes if it's not at someone else's expense. The Peacemaker Soul has a really hard time being selfish, and feels the need to be always compromising, which can be both irritating and frustrating to those around who love this soul. It can also be easy for people, even those same loving and caring people, to take advantage of this soul. However, this is not a soul you should underestimate, for if really pushed to the limit they will show their teeth, even if only for a moment.

From the energy group of Water, the Peacemaker will strive to please, to compromise in whatever way they can. Always looking to the left, always looking to the right, always wanting to do the right thing, and often at their own expense.

Character Traits of the Peacemaker Soul

Quiet, tranquil, serene, mentally calm, evaluating in all things. Hates war or conflict and will often do anything, even at their own expense, to keep the peace; sometimes heads toward martyrdom. Believes in freedom of speech and can be an activist, but is always compromising. Very friendly but also very shy, is conciliatory and has a need to belong. Is a good mediator, a true negotiator, an assenter, a moderator—makes a good therapist or counselor. Is a pacifist and an intermediary—could become a missionary or volunteer.

The Peacemaker Soul needs to give and take, likes to and indeed has a need to reconcile differences. Is extremely diplomatic and generally gives good advice. Would make a good referee or politician. Often a go-between, makes a good matchmaker or marriage broker. Is an excellent spokesperson, very good in public relations, will weigh situations fairly, is a good consultant. Has a tendency to be quietly judgmental, but can also be sensitive, gentle, giving, concerned, and caring of others. Uncaring of rights and wrongs, is very trusting and also trustworthy. Has a higher sense of truth, can be selfless to the point of self damage. Has a good sense of humor, can be very creative, likes music and books. Has a retentive mind, especially when it comes to remembering people and situations.

RELATIONSHIPS AND THE PEACEMAKER SOUL

In a mate, the Peacemaker is looking mostly for someone who is sensitive and able to "tune in" to their wavelength. Does not need an argumentative or disruptive person but will often be drawn to such in their need to be valued as a moderator. Needs a mate who allows them a voice and who has a good sense of fairness and honesty.

DANGERS: Being used as a pawn in other people's arguments; expecting others to have the same sense of values, as this can lead to great disappointments; can become a doormat.

SONG OF THE PEACEMAKER SOUL

The Peacemaker is matched to the Jonquilla, which has the common name Rising Star. The Jonquil is one of the most loved of the daffodils, as is its soul match, the wonderful Peacemaker Soul, who is quiet, tranquil, and mentally calm.

The Old Soul

I think that most of us, at some point in our lives, have met or known an Old Soul. Fairly easy to recognize, usually compromising and willing to listen, the Old Soul has a quiet sense of knowing which will draw those seeking sound advice. An Old Soul can always be relied on in times of real crisis.

From the energy group of Water, the Old Soul is driven by an energy force that inspires and drives them to evaluate and compromise, often in the extreme. This can drive them to tie themselves in knots, as they want so badly to make the right decisions in life, which will freeze them into nonaction sometimes. I have a good friend who is obviously a Water sign, and her behavior is so comically that of her type that she just can't help it. When we are together and I hear her say, "Should I, or shouldn't I? I can't quite decide. . . . If I do that . . ." I start to grin, she sees me, and we laugh.

CHARACTER TRAITS OF THE OLD SOUL

Knowledgeable, practiced, spiritual, advanced. Can be conservative, appreciates tradition. Open, very loyal, can be tolerant of many things but also extremely intolerant and judgmental at times. Can be a creature of habit. Is prepared for most things, always deducing and evaluating. Mellow, wise, likes company but also likes to be alone. Seemingly contradictory in nature; likes order, even in chaos; is compromising, yet uncompromising of right action; is sensible, feet on the ground, usually patient, but will be impatient of what they perceive as trivial, dishonest, or unfair behavior.

The Old Soul is able to join in any conversation, is interested in most subjects, and is a good listener. Takes a while to make friends. Cranial knowledge can get in the way of the knowing instinct sometimes. Is the kind of person people come to for advice. Extremely determined and hardworking, rarely seeks conflict but will stand their ground if forced into a fight, and will more quickly fight for the rights of others rather than for themselves. Hates injustice, is very protective of family and close friends. Can be demanding of right behavior from others. Doesn't sweat the small stuff and much prefers larger and more complex challenges. Relates especially to the young and the old.

RELATIONSHIPS AND THE OLD SOUL

The Old Soul is extremely independent and capable of living alone, but likes companionship and so leans toward long-term relationships or marriage. Needs a mate who is loyal and has high moral standards. Likes stability at home and at work, and so the most incompatible soul might be the Traveler Soul. One of the most compatible souls might be the Newborn— someone to take care of, to enjoy, and who offers a fresh and new perspective which the Old Soul takes pleasure in sharing.

DANGERS: Becoming irritated and impatient; too controlling; easily frustrated by what is perceived as stupid or ignorant behavior; holding others to their own high standards.

Song of the Old Soul

The Old Soul is matched to the Long-cupped daffodil, and as we look at this remarkable bloom, we can immediately see the worth of this soul. White with the purity of age, its pale-pink center speaks of the energy of love. Its petals fall back, exposing its heart, leaving it open and trusting and very, very brave.

Our last group is one that we would rather not have in our soul cluster. It is certainly not one of God. However, it is that one soul we need to know about, to be aware of, above all others. Let us deal with it now and know its face: The Dark Soul.

The Dark Soul

Very few of us would say we know such a soul as the Dark Soul; however, it is difficult to be certain, as the cunning nature of this soul helps it hide, and we will rarely be able to recognize it unless or until some terrible dark shadow falls upon us, at which time the harm would be done.

From the energy group of Sulphur, the Dark Soul is driven to action purely by the influence of evil. The Dark Soul will destroy and disrupt, and will savor each and every dark moment.

Unlike the other four energy groups, which each contain three very individual soul signs, each using the same energy but differently, there is only one soul sign in the Sulphur group, although we could say that there are three different levels and types of power: two obvious and extreme, one more balanced and much less obvious, all of them Dark but with differing intensity and shades.

CHARACTER TRAITS OF THE DARK SOUL

Evil, sinister, always buried in dark thoughts; sullen, angry, will constantly be mired in a dark mood. Secretive, mysterious, unenlightened—there is an absence of light. Sly, mean, extremely spiteful, cunning, hateful, shrouded and despising of all things that shed light. Lives on the dark side, never thinks of others except in how they can be used, completely self-absorbed, cruel, black hearted, malevolent, immoral, damning, damned, wicked, demonic. Discontent, sullen, quick to outbursts of anger. Corrupt.

The Dark Soul will willingly commit heinous acts against anyone, even those close to them. Vicious, base, foul, shameless, vile, obscene, fiendish. Some may be referred to as fallen angels. Excited by sinful acts, a Dark Soul is a soul who has come to this earth to revel in and to enjoy the act of corruption, who has and who will *intentionally* manipulate in order to destroy light and truth and goodness, who will feed long and greedily on the fears of all creatures.

RELATIONSHIPS AND THE DARK SOUL

A Dark Soul has the need to stay hidden and will, through great cunning, find many willing victims as their prey. No relationship with this soul will be lasting, and all who form a bond will be damaged beyond recognition as they will try to corrupt all who come in close contact. A Dark Soul despises light and will look for a way to extinguish it, often through defiling or causing death.

DANGERS: Coming up against a soul who is pure light and incorruptible.

Song of the Dark Soul

The Dark Soul is not included among our host of beautiful daffodils, yet it does have a flower, there is a spirit, an aura emitted from this soul; but the spirit of the Dark Soul is not a golden or bright thing. It lives among us, though, and has the potential to grow, just as we do, and it can invade our garden without our being immediately aware of its existence. Its flower? Later, you will see.

GOING WITH THE FLOW

We now know about all thirteen soul signs. We know which elemental forces influence and drive them, and, therefore, which group each sign belongs in. We have a detailed picture of their character traits. We have a general idea of how they relate to others in a relationship. And we can see in our mind's eye how each soul's bloom—each except the Dark Soul—is represented in the natural world by a beautiful and unique flower.

All of these should help you identify your own soul sign. But what if you're still not sure which is you? Then it will be illuminating to consider another aspect of the human cluster of souls: energy flow. By understanding how energy moves inward and outward from each of the elemental groups, we can gain additional insight into each of the soul signs and, in turn, our unique destiny.

Energy flow influences how we process our thoughts, view our lives, approach our experiences, and handle ourselves. Energy flows through us, like a permanent electric current; it is within us, we cannot help but be driven by it. It is the force that gives breath to our soul, life to our soul—it is our life force. We can learn to stem the tide, to hold it back, or to let it flow through us, uninhibited. Once we understand that we have this power and how it works, we can use it consciously to great effect. So what kind of energy are we talking about, and what effect do the three different styles of energy have on our soul signs?

Within each pocket, each elemental energy group, energy ebbs and flows, moving generally in a circular movement. If we think of it like looking at an ultrasound of a child in a mother's womb, we see the child surrounded by fluids which protect and nurture the child, maintaining an environment that encourages development. It's the same way with the energy that surrounds, protects, and encourages the development of each unique soul. Within the spiritual sac, our celestial membrane, our amniotic energy is what builds the eyes, the ears, the heart, and the depth and breadth of our soul. Depending on what part of the sac, the energy pocket, we lie in, certain currents of energy affect us more than others, infusing our soul. The outer regions of the pocket are where the elemental energy is most extreme, most obvious, and most obviously changing, whereas the central part of the pocket has an energy that's more dense, with seemingly less movement.

And so while energy flows within each soul group, it also flows inward and outward to affect each soul sign in a particular way. In each pocket we have one soul sign influenced by an inflowing, or Introvert, energy; another influenced by an outflowing, or Extrovert, energy; and one soul sign influenced by a Central energy, capable naturally of flowing both ways.

As we talk about Introvert or Extrovert energy, we have to be careful not to assume that a person with an Introvert energy necessarily has an introverted personality, or that someone who has an Extrovert energy necessarily has an extroverted personality. We are talking here about energy flow, about the movement and direction that our natural-born energy flows through us and determines our thought process and the way in which we act.

A soul sign with an Introvert energy flow tends toward the type of thinking and reasoning we associate with a subjective thought process. A soul sign with a Central energy flow tends to think and to reason in a more balanced way, able to flow either to a subjective or an objective thought process. And a soul sign with an Extrovert energy flow tends toward the type of thinking and reasoning we associate with an objective thought process.

So how do we know which soul signs have an Introvert flow, which have a Central flow, and which have an Extrovert flow? It's easy. The chart below shows how each of these flows occurs in a reliable pattern, from left to right, within each of the energy groups.

ENERGY GROUP	INTROVERT	CENTRAL	EXTROVERT
◯ FIRE	*Retrospective*	*Dreaming*	*Bright Star*
⊕ EARTH	*Hunter*	*Visionary*	*Warrior*
⊙ AIR	*Traveler*	*Prophet*	*Newborn*
⊖ WATER	*Seeker*	*Peacemaker*	*Old*
⚥ SULPHUR	*Dark*	*Dark*	*Dark*

At a glance we can see our energy group, where our soul sign occurs in the group, and whether our energy flow is Introvert, Central, or Extrovert. This is the chart by which we can know the human soul cluster.

Describing the placement of each soul sign in its own group, I use the term *extreme* to describe the left and right energy forces, meaning that the force and flow—the power—of these energies are more obvious, more outwardly apparent to us. More importantly, the chart shows us that the force of these energies is flowing in opposite directions.

Then we have that central, more balanced and even energy flow, able to move with ease, to flow naturally either to the left or the right or stay centered. Central souls are able to use their energy force in a less obvious but equally powerful way as their more extreme sister souls, flowing easily and smoothly, staying more in balance with their elemental force.

It's important to know that no one energy flow is more desirable, more powerful, or better than another, just different, allowing our character traits to bloom in different ways and in different circumstances, giving each soul a unique sense of direction and purpose, helping to make us the individuals that we are.

So what are those differences? In what way does our particular energy flow influence us? Let's look at each of the energy groups and their soul signs in detail.

We see that the five soul signs on the extreme left of the chart—The Retrospective Soul, The Hunter Soul, The Traveler Soul, The Seeker Soul, and The Dark Soul—have an Introvert energy flow, which manifests in each of these five souls as a person who has difficulty expressing inner personal feelings, who prefers to hold back, to keep something of themselves in reserve.

Out of all the Fire signs, the **Retrospective Soul** finds it most difficult to compromise. They so badly want the dream, the knight in shining armor, the fairy-tale ending. Because they are driven by this extreme emotional energy, wearing their heart on their sleeve, their actions and attitudes show their disappointment. Nothing is right because nothing is as perfect as they had dreamed it would be.

The **Hunter Soul** may seem to be extroverted but often hides their true self, internalizing their quest to fulfill their own needs. It's actually a strong internal drive, to be able to really figure out what they want in life and to go and get it. Our Hunter can be either extremely positive or extremely negative, with the extreme left energy force driving them in a very obvious way, depending, of course, on the circumstances. Driven by the need to take action through strategy, they will need to feel in control, often showing that extreme energy, and planning and strategizing, all the way.

The **Traveler Soul**, also, seems in some ways to be influenced by Extrovert energy. The Traveler is certainly not intimidated by others, and that strength comes from internalizing, doing what they want to do. This is probably the most complex sign in the Air group, coming from the extreme left energy force, and will be the most likely of the three to show any aggressive behavior. It takes a lot to get our Traveler to this point, as that passive-aggressive nature will only show itself if an Air sign has grown up in an oppressed environment, or if constant nagging, bullying, or oppressive behavior of someone continually and over a period of time forces their will. Then all three soul signs may be driven to take an action, to a greater or lesser extent, depending where in the chart they occur. Our Traveler will have a more difficult time than the others in this group as far as relationships go, and has a tendency to be more afraid of personal commitment than either the Prophet or the Newborn. Not necessarily a bad thing, but it can definitely create problems in certain areas of their lives.

The **Seeker Soul**, if you remember, can be fascinating, an interesting person to meet at a party, certainly not shy or inhibited. Yet as far as emotions go, this soul is reserved, holds back, doesn't easily commit, has a difficult time taking responsibility for anyone but themselves, and will make sure their own needs are met before they can take care of others' needs. These are internal characteristics. The Seeker soul, driven by that extreme left energy force, is extremely strong willed, and although it is in their natural-born energy to compromise, they will use their incredible reasoning skills to evaluate a situation to their way of thinking, if they can.

The **Dark Soul**, influenced by this extreme Introvert energy, will internalize, harbor grudges, hold feelings inside, and then explode, staying angry and self-absorbed.

It could be said that Introvert energy manifests as selfishness, but there's more to it than that. I would say that Introvert energy manifests as a person knowing and also needing self-interest, who has a tendency to apply judgments or conclusions of most situations based on how they perceive they might act, react, or feel in that same situation. Looking to self first, and internalizing, then able to look beyond self, and to broaden their view—this is their natural-born flow, this is the direction they instinctively take. Their direction is subjective.

If we look again at the chart, we can see that the five souls on the extreme right—The Bright Star Soul, The Warrior Soul, The Newborn Soul, The Old Soul, and, again, The Dark Soul—have an Extrovert energy flow, which manifests in each of the five souls as a person who is able to acknowledge their inner feelings, and because of this cannot help but have a wide focus, to give openly in a less uninhibited way.

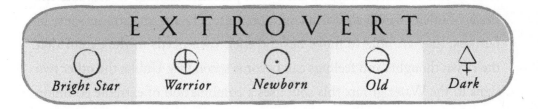

The **Bright Star Soul** is the most positively and obviously expressive of emotions among the Fire signs. The Bright Star has difficulty sometimes, though, with discipline and can be indiscreet and way too sharing with their personal life at inappropriate moments. Their heart may be as big and as open as can be, but they will have real difficulty being thoughtful, and will express their thoughts and feelings in a heartbeat.

The **Warrior Soul**'s natural inclination is to look outside themselves, look out for the good of the whole—their troops, their family, other people in their care. They will reach beyond their own needs, even to their own detriment. Their energy, like the Hunter, is more obvious than the Visionary, the central force figure.

The **Newborn Soul**, who simply cannot hold anything back—what you see is what you get—is practically unable to disguise their feelings. Open and trusting, friendly and warmhearted, sociable and enthusiastic, they find it difficult to keep a secret because of their natural inclination toward an extrovert flow of energy, toward expressing themselves. The energy force of passive, gentle flow drives them forward, and they are rarely discontent, even when dealing with a more aggressive or demanding soul sign.

The **Old Soul**, who does not necessarily have an extroverted personality, is truly able to extend beyond their own personal feelings to evaluate the needs of others wisely and with common sense. Having an extreme sense of fairness, they are able to move beyond their own needs to the extent that their own thoughts and feelings can become secondary. Unlike the other two signs in the Water group, this soul uses a combination of extreme common sense and gut instinct. So no matter how a situation may seem to be, evaluating from all sides, an Old Soul, often even without realizing it, will use their instincts, will sense something within a situation which is not necessarily obvious and will take this knowing into their calculations. An office manager, for example, needing to create a happy workplace, will sense a disruptive personality, even if it is not apparent to others. Then they will find a way either to accept or to change the way that person or situation is, through compromise.

The **Dark Soul**, influenced by this extreme Extrovert energy, will externalize, will have difficulty holding back, and will have a need to show themselves, to be seen for who they are.

It could be said that Extrovert energy manifests as selflessness. I would say that this energy manifests as a person who simply cannot help but be open, who has a tendency to apply judgments or conclusions of most situations based on their ability to look beyond the internal, to have a wider vision, a broader perception and more outgoing view of other's actions and reactions, related to their own.

Now, looking at the chart once more, we can see that the five souls in the center—The Dreaming Soul, The Visionary Soul, The Prophet Soul, The Peacemaker Soul, and, yet again, The Dark Soul—have a central and therefore more balanced energy flow that manifests as a person who can move or flow quite easily into the stream of energy from either left or right, who can be influenced to a degree by extreme Introvert energy, or extreme Extrovert energy, but who will not usually be an extreme individual but rather a more balanced and reasoning soul.

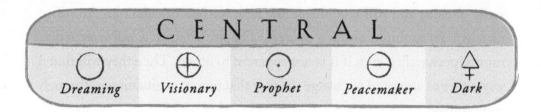

CENTRAL

Dreaming   Visionary   Prophet   Peacemaker   Dark

The **Dreaming Soul** internalizes things but is able to avoid negative behavior. Still, as a Fire sign, their emotions are powerful but not obvious to an untrained observer. Artistic and creative, the Dreaming Soul has a lot going on in their head, and, influenced by that somewhat uncompromising and willful energy to the left, will find ingenious and often unusual ways to expression of self. Because they are much more able to be creative with their emotions than the Retrospective Soul, and again, having a central, and therefore more balanced force of energy, most Dreaming souls are, unlike the Retrospective Soul, quite content with life.

The **Visionary Soul**, with incredible instincts and insightfulness, is able to see both sides of a coin, to negotiate, to mediate, act as the perfect go-between or referee. Like the other souls influenced by this kinder, gentler Central energy, the Visionary will be slow to make harsh judgments, and can be lenient and neutral in most arguments. Driven by the same Earth energy as the other two signs in the group, this soul uses that energy in a much different way. As the central and therefore more balanced sign in the group, the Visionary's energy is shown in a much more subtle and far less demanding way, and because of this their power will go unnoticed by many.

The **Prophet Soul**, who does not waste time or energy worrying about the rights or wrongs of any given situation, is always able to see all points of view, able to flow into the stream of energy which can take them into the flow of both extremes, while remaining balanced and held in place by their own Central energy force. As such, they are able to not get caught up or trapped by extreme energy. Usually evenly balanced emotionally, the Prophet is the most balanced soul in the well-balanced Air group.

The **Peacemaker Soul,** who unlike the Prophet Soul does get caught up and tangled at times, feels the tugging of those extreme currents of energy and must continually strive to keep a balance—or, rather, to keep the peace. The Peacemaker is still a very powerful mediator or negotiator, as the ability to see both sides of the coin, and the need to compromise and to keep the peace, holds them to a definite sense of fair play. Very family oriented, the Peacemaker will do almost anything to make their family happy. And they make it work. In the workplace they are quietly confident.

The **Dark Soul,** also influenced by this Central and more balanced energy, at times can be temperate and seem emotionally balanced. This works to the Dark Soul's advantage, as their evil power is then less likely to be detected.

It could be said that Central energy manifests as an energy that is diffused, diluted, less powerful. I would say that this energy manifests as a person who, when in stressful situations, simply cannot help but be a fence-sitter. They will try to be reasonable, nonextremist, and will have a tendency to apply judgments or conclusions in most situations based on their ability to stay neutral, to put themselves into the shoes of others, to experience all degrees of energy flow, and to have a less than judgmental view of others, actions and reactions. This is their natural-born flow, this is the direction they instinctively take.

It is important to note yet again that the Sulphur group is unlike the other four groups, having only one soul sign, the Dark Soul. I think all of us will know, without explanation, the meaning and character traits implied by "The Dark Soul." However, we would be foolish to ignore this soul sign, as the Dark Soul does play a significant role in our human existence here on this earth, which I will detail in a coming chapter. Just as in the other primary soul groups, there is an extreme left energy, an extreme right energy, and a more balanced energy in between in the Sulphur pocket. But depending on what energy they are influenced by—Introvert, Extrovert, or Central—there are three varying degrees of the Dark Soul, each one equally powerful: two who have a very obvious and intense energy flow; one, just as intense, but much more hidden, much less obvious. Having the energy of pure evil, Dark Souls are driven to create darkness and despair, pain and suffering, and can be very cunning, very sly, often moving among us undetected, and we rarely know of them until they strike. Often a loner, the Dark Soul will readily join with others of their kind if it suits their evil purpose. Finally, Dark Souls are relatively few in number, although just one among us is one too many for me.

NAILING IT DOWN

Most of you by now recognize your soul group and your soul sign. How do I know this? Because I have seen it work again and again. But there are those of you who need a little more—you know, or you think you know, but you need confirmation. This chapter is meant to provide it.

Just as we did with the energy groups in Part II, we are going to use a variety of examples of actions to help clarify the soul signs. Just as with our soul groups, you may want to choose more than one likely action: "Well, that would be me, but that would also be me." Because each of the three soul signs in each group is infused with and powered by the same type of energy, you will probably say yes to at least two of the responses, but you need to ask yourself this question: Which response is more me? Let me give you an example of what I'm saying.

My daughter, Samantha Jane, and I are in the same soul group. I am a Warrior and she is a Visionary. One of the main reasons that we have such a great relationship is because we are both Earth signs and we each can really understand where the other is coming from. It also helps that she is a Central and therefore balanced soul, and I am an Extreme soul. When we get into the chapter on relationships you'll understand better how that works.

It was easy for me to know myself as a Warrior Soul, as Grey Eagle told me so. Samantha, though, was a whole different story. When she read each of the descriptions of the three choices in her group—the Warrior Soul, the Visionary Soul, and the Hunter Soul—she knew right then that she was a Visionary, although there were one or two traits which she said were not her. That was easy to explain. Our environment, our upbringing, encourages us to develop some character traits more than others, and she was perfectly at ease with that, knowing that so much of the description was right. Then, like the rest of us, she looked for confirmation, and for me this was great, as I used her as one of my guinea pigs, knowing she would be very vocal if I was off the mark.

As a Visionary Soul, she considered the final set of questions that applied to the Earth signs: Are you the kind of person who is always the first to volunteer for even the most difficult of tasks, those tasks which no one else might want? And, are you the kind of person who will call friends, make plans to get together, organize social events, even when those friends don't call you?

We both answered yes to each question, and there is no doubt that my daughter would volunteer to do all kinds of things, although not as naturally or readily as I would. I do organize get-togethers, call friends, etc., but not to nearly the same degree as my daughter does.

So which is most like you? If you mostly—but not always—relate to the following statements that describe a particular soul sign, then you've found your sign.

If you are a **Fire** sign, do you

- Sometimes feel negative and often find something to complain about?

- Find that you are either extremely encouraging or extremely discouraging of others and their actions?

- Dream of the perfect mate even though you are disappointed again and again when others let you down?

If this sounds most like you, then you are a **Retrospective Soul**.

Or do you

- Feel compelled to express your artistic temperament?

- Think you are sometimes unrealistic about your expectations of people and situations?

- Find that you often look through rose-colored glasses to try to see only the best in someone?

If this sounds most like you, then you are a **Dreaming Soul**.

Or do you

- Think of yourself as positive and outgoing, especially in difficult circumstances?

- Love to be center stage, even if it is at the expense of others?

- Need accolades and a partner who gives you their full attention?

If this sounds most like you, then you are a **Bright Star Soul**.

Or, if you are an **Earth** sign, do you

- Love a challenge and strive to conquer it at all costs?

- Motivate others with your enthusiasm but move on if they hold you up or disrupt your plans?

- Need freedom and flexibility in any personal relationship?

If this sounds most like you, then you are a **Hunter Soul**.

Or do you

- Take a while to decide on the right career path?

- Think of yourself as a social organizer who will call others even if they don't call you?

- Need reassurance and security, as you're not always sure of your own value?

If this sounds most like you, then you are a **Visionary Soul**.

Or do you

- Naturally take charge of most situations?

- Find that you are usually the first one to volunteer?

- Need to be involved with your partner and have real communication?

If this sounds most like you, then you are a **Warrior Soul**.

Or, if you are an **Air** sign, do you

- Very often wonder if the grass might be greener someplace other than where you are?

- Not really *need* the security of a house, home, or family?

- Consider yourself romantic and love the idea of romance but find it difficult to commit to a single relationship?

If this sounds most like you, then you are a **Traveler Soul**.

Or do you

- Feel content to be wherever you are at any given moment?

- Avoid conflict of any kind in order to keep stability both at home and at work?

- Need a stable partner who is totally committed to you, even if the relationship is not perfect?

If this sounds most like you, then are a **Prophet Soul**.

Or do you

- Need the opportunity to try out new and innovative ideas?

- Value stability and almost always feel like things *are* stable?

- Openly and easily share your emotions, and need a grounded home life?

If this sounds most like you, then you are a **Newborn Soul**.

Or, if you are a **Water** sign, do you

- Always find yourself interested in others?

- Like to involve yourself with worthwhile projects, and love to philosophize and intellectualize things?

- Want a relationship, but like to hold back, and find it hard to share inner feelings?

If this sounds most like you, then you are a **Seeker Soul**.

Or do you

- Feel like your main focus is on marriage and family, even on social occasions?

- Work with children, or in a teaching, caring, or nurturing profession?

- Enjoy nurturing your family?

If this sounds most like you, then you are a **Peacemaker Soul**.

Or do you

- Like company, but feel you can be just as happy doing your own thing by yourself?

- Get involved with several projects at once, finding it hard to say no?

- Like to make the rules in your relationship?

If this sounds most like you, then you are an **Old Soul**.

When we look at how our learned behavior can change our natural inclinations, and when we apply a large amount of real honesty about ourselves, we inevitably come to the right conclusion.

Some of you know yourselves perfectly well and will instantly recognize your soul sign. Some of you will struggle, perhaps because it might be hard to accept some things about yourselves, or because you don't fully realize which of your traits are negative and which are positive. Some of you may have low self-esteem and find it hard to accept the good things while more easily accepting the bad.

A good friend of mine immediately knew her soul group, and then, reading the descriptions of her three soul-sign choices, was able to dismiss one of them pretty quickly. The other two choices she had some difficulty with; she went back and forth between them for a while.

Her difficulty stemmed not from her ability to accept those traits that might be considered negative, but those traits she had always attributed to people "more clever than me."

Inventive, innovative, original, artistic, creative, likes to be a trendsetter—these were traits she saw far more readily in others than in herself. Her low self-esteem, her humility, was clouding her judgment of herself, as it does with so many of us. Her friends could easily recognize those traits in her, but she needed to see them for herself.

"Well," she said to me, "I'm not a bit artistic. I don't paint, and I couldn't draw to save my life. That is definitely not me."

"Oh, so who makes your clothes, who sews, who makes those fabulous drapes you have? Who cooks, develops new recipes, is always trying new things?"

Inventive, innovative, original? You should see her outfits. Artistic, creative? She's always wearing something unusual and different. Her home is beautiful—she has an eye for the unusual and is not afraid to be a trendsetter, no matter how shy, no matter how little self-esteem she has. But it was difficult at first for her to see these things in herself.

As soon as I began pointing some of these things out to her, my friend realized that she had been looking at herself in a very narrow way. She needed to broaden her view. Very easy when it came to others, hard when it came to viewing herself.

Many of us are like that. We find it far easier to see the negatives as opposed to the positives in our nature, often because we have been brought up in an environment that did not encourage us to value who we are.

Another friend of mine, one of the most kind and gentle of souls, was married for thirty-nine years to an arrogant, overbearing, bullying, and very mean individual who sapped her energy and destroyed her self-esteem. He is a Fire sign, the most negative kind of Retrospective Soul. Disillusioned and angry with his life, he blamed everything that went wrong on his wife. He didn't just walk all over her, he pounded her into the ground. She, from the Air-influenced group, passive and gentle, was the most loyal and devoted wife, always trying to see the good in him, always making excuses to others for his arrogance and bad behavior.

It was easy for Eileen to see which group she belonged to. She was well aware of her passive nature, but it was very difficult for her to accept that those truly wonderful traits that all Air signs have applied to her. She had been so used to being told that she was worthless, she actually believed it.

She recently came to stay with me, and one morning I was complaining that I'd had a really dreadful night's sleep.

"Oh, Rosemary," she whispered, "was it something I did?"

Now, how sad is that?

It can be hard for some of us to see ourselves as others see us. We are not always used to being honest about ourselves, about our true feelings. Sometimes it hurts too much. But we are all of us souls in God's garden, and He sees us just as we are. Each of us a small and delicate flower, blowing this way and that in a sea of souls, doing the best that we can. Twelve beautiful blooms, golden like the daffodil, shimmering and bright.

And yet . . . And yet there is one other, a flower among us that tries its best to bring harm to our garden of souls.

EVIL IN OUR MIDST

A worm, a grub, a slug . . . something harmless in our garden grows? I wish, I wish, I wish.

We know by now that there is one soul group left, one soul sign we have not yet fully spoken of, one I would rather ignore. But I can't. I am not allowed, for unfortunately our garden would not be complete without it, the last of our thirteen soul signs, that Dark Soul, which is very much a part of our soul cluster. This is a fact we have to face.

I have seen evil many times in my work as a spiritual medium, and I have written of my experiences with evil from time to time, but I didn't really understand the existence of evil in the universe until Grey Eagle told me about soul signs. I had always believed, always wanted to believe, that God was in all of us, in all things. But I was wrong—there is such a thing as absolute evil, an energy darker than anything we can imagine.

Before we take a look at Dark Souls and their dark deeds, I would like to clarify the difference between an evil soul created from Sulphur energy—a true Dark Soul—and a soul created from one of the other four elemental energy groups who commits evil acts but not a Dark Soul.

We all are capable of committing a dark act, and most of us do, more often than we should. A dark act can be as inconsequential as snapping at someone in temper, saying something mean or unkind about another person, or deliberately withholding affection or compliments. We are all capable of saying and doing bad things, even though the vast majority of us come from one of the four energy sources that God created. Any act born of meanness, spite, or unkindness, no matter how small, casts a shadow over our soul. For most of us, though, the shadows that are cast are not from evil intent but born of frustration and lack of tolerance. This doesn't make it right, and we can't dilute the consequences—people are still hurt as a result of our actions, and we are hurt as a result of our actions. This is part of our learning and growth process.

But what about thieves, murderers, rapists, and other violent criminals? What about those cultures that seem to promote brutal behavior toward women? What about religions or belief systems that seem to promote retribution?

It is possible, due to upbringing, environment, or cultural or religious conditioning, for a soul born of God to be influenced, swayed toward living on the shadow side. It can happen to anyone. If we are so encouraged, and if we choose, it can be easy to develop that small dark side, that capacity for spite and ill will. But it cannot entirely take us over, for nothing can extinguish entirely the God force, that force of light within. Even though the force can be repressed, it will show itself, even if in only one small act of love. The love of a child, a wife, or a husband; the love of a plant, a bird, or nature in general. The fact that we can love at all, even if only in the smallest way, shows the light of God.

Dark Souls cannot love. They may seem to love, but in fact they *revel*. Dark Souls revel in, delight in, immerse themselves in their evil nature. They revel in the force of destruction, the power of their evil, their intention to do evil. Dark Souls are incapable of true contrition, or of any real feelings of guilt or remorse. They revel in their dark acts and are incapable of love, even in the smallest degree.

A man who commits murder may go home to his wife and child, whom he loves, and they see him only as a decent father and husband. The ability of a Dark Soul to disguise himself? No—because he loves, his evil is not the act of a Dark Soul but that of a soul of light gone dark.

A woman has five children, four she loves and treats fairly. The fifth she dislikes, treats meanly, abuses. The four see her as a wonderful mother, which to them she truly is. The fifth child is emotionally damaged and has extremely low self-esteem, blaming herself for not being good enough for her mother to love. The mother knows this and revels in her power over the child. But . . . she loves. Her evil is not that of a Dark Soul but of a soul of light gone dark.

A child is given everything: a safe home, caring teachers, a warm and happy family. She uses them, is able very easily to take advantage, is born with no conscience and is incapable of love or affection; yet outwardly she acts sweet and kind and generous. Using people is a dark act; having no conscience about it and being incapable of love or affection is the mark of a true Dark Soul. Acting sweet and kind is the devious action of a Dark Soul wanting to disguise its true self—a bad seed.

And so there is evil out there, Dark Souls who walk among us, souls who have sunk their roots into the earth, who feed from the same source, drink from the same well, and who grow and flower, just as the rest of us do, in the same garden of souls. But their flower is different than the rest of us, and if I could, I would weed them out one by one and destroy them all. But I cannot, for I am a lowly gardener who does not understand God's master plan. And as much as I might dig and weed and water, I am only a small, small bloom in a garden greater than I can imagine.

I have been asked many times over the last two years at talks and seminars about why God would allow such a presence among us. My answer, based on my twenty-plus years of experience, is this: I have, too many times, seen the results wrought on our human race by the evil forces of darkness. But I have also seen the courage, the strength, and the inner power of those who have been most affected by this evil. When something gets taken away from us, God always gives us something back. If we never experienced the effects of evil upon us, our growth, our light, our power, would never have the opportunity to expand. Evil, as terrible as it is, is necessary in our midst, and God allows it for the sake of our souls.

History is full of examples of evil men, obvious Dark Souls: Ivan the Terrible, Genghis Khan, Pol Pot, Joseph Stalin, Adolf Hitler. More recently we experienced the anguish caused by terrorists such as Osama Bin Laden, who has brought darkness and shadow into what we all thought was a safe and secure existence. We know these names well. All had political as well as personal agendas; they were leaders of men, leaders of nations, influencing, encouraging, and driving their followers to participate in their terrible and vile plots, reveling in and committed to the power of evil over good. Our world still rocks from the effects of their evil.

Then there are those who acted on a smaller but no less horrific scale, serial killers such as Jack the Ripper, the Boston Strangler, Hamilton Albert Fish (the real-life model for Hannibal "The Cannibal" Lechter), Elizabeth "The Countess of Transylvania" Báthory, John Wayne Gacy, Jeffrey Dahmer, and David "Son of Sam" Berkowitz. Other names we connect with evil and darkness: Timothy McVeigh, Reverend Jim Jones, Charles Manson, and Ted Bundy—a perfect example, it would seem, of a Dark Soul.

Were these people, and others like them, mentally insane, warped by an abusive childhood, or simply born evil? And what of child and teen criminals, such as Columbine High School gunmen Dylan Klebold and Eric Harris? Many of these have come from good and loving homes. Are these children unaccountably evil for no reason? Or are they souls of light gone bad? Flowers that bloom only in the dark? Bad seeds? Dark Souls?

Psychologists have been debating the nature-versus-nurture issue forever. I think both play a part, but there is more, much more to it than that.

As we are learning, not everyone who commits an evil act is a Dark Soul. There are many, through some quirk of nature and an extreme negative response to their nurturing, who act out in anger and defiance. Some, influenced by their peers, are driven by self-righteous causes, at the heart of which is fear. A hatred of blacks, of Jews, of homosexuals, of abortion—yes, there are many who have committed heinous acts, despicable and evil crimes against others in the name of righteousness, in the name of God. There are also those who react extremely to a specific situation: Susan Smith, the South Carolina woman who drowned her two young sons by strapping them into the family car and rolling it into a lake, apparently to appear less encumbered to a boyfriend; and Andrea Yates, the Texas mother convicted of drowning five of her children in the bathtub, who had reportedly been suffering from depression. In some of these acts, souls of light stray into the dark side; in others we see the actions of a Dark Soul.

Prior to our birth here on earth, it is decided that we will be placed into an environment that is best suited to our potential growth. We begin a journey which gives us countless experiences, and countless choices. Those born of the light, who choose to stray into their dark side, do so by choice. No matter how abusive and terrible our upbringing, no matter what reasons we might find to justify going bad, there is always a choice: to do unto others what has been done unto you, or to learn what it means to suffer and as a result become committed to a better way of life.

We try to figure it out, to reason why someone would choose the dark path. We want to call them insane, to justify their horrendous actions as mad, to make it easier on ourselves. But I know differently, and as much as I would like not to know, and as much as I might agree with the medical profession that insanity does exist, and as much as I agree with the Church that evil forces do use those too weak to resist, I *do* know that there are those, born of light, of God, which evil forces can and do possess. I also know that those same evil forces are capable of producing and indeed do produce souls of darkness and evil who come to this earth, as do we all, to learn and to grow—but these endeavor to learn how to be more dark.

There are three of them, three different kinds, three different degrees of the Dark Soul, as you have seen looking at our chart: one, an Introvert energy; one, a balanced, Central energy; and one, an Extrovert energy. None is more dangerous than another, as each has equal power, as do the rest of us in our soul groups. However, two are more obvious energies, and one is more hidden.

The Dark Soul influenced and created from an Introvert energy will tend toward a brooding and selfish personality. They may appear to be mysterious and secretive, which can be a great attraction to some people, and may well be seen by the opposite sex as a fascinating challenge. The Introvert Dark Soul knows this and will use this power to full advantage.

The Dark Soul influenced and created from a Central energy will tend toward a more normal personality. They can appear to be reasonable, thoughtful, and interested in others' welfare, which will attract those who have issues with self-worth or are looking for support during a difficult time in their lives. The Central-energy Dark Soul will know this and will prey on the sensitivity and vulnerability of their victim.

The Dark Soul influenced and created from Extrovert energy will tend to be friendly and outgoing, often gregarious and fun loving, which will attract those looking for something new and exciting in their lives. The Extrovert energy Dark Soul will know this and revel in the challenge of the conquest.

Part of our garden of souls, a Dark Soul is just as the rest of us, like a flower bulb with roots that sink into the earth, with the same need for nourishment, and with the same potential to bloom, to flourish. But what kind of bulb, what type of flower, could such evil produce? If we could picture it, what flower would we see?

Not surprisingly, there is such a bulb, and Grey Eagle has led me to it. *Dracunculus vulgaris* resembles an oversize blood-red calla lily with a long black spadix, the fleshy spike that thrusts up from the base of the hood. Tiny flowers that are hidden from view give off a smell that one of my gardening books calls "disgusting."

If we look at this bloom closely, we can see how clearly the *Dracunculus* resembles the Dark Soul. It blooms at the base, *base* also meaning without honor or decency, ignoble, contemptible, mean, and degrading; its flowers remain hidden from view, as the truly Dark Soul will hide its energy; the spadix reflects the Dark Soul's black heart; and, if we could smell evil, the stench from this bulb might be what we would smell.

It is hard to imagine that any flower should bear such a name, *Dracunculus*, but there it is. I look at the flower, and although I don't want to, I can actually see a kind of beauty and realize why some souls of light might be drawn to this type of energy. The Dracunculus relies on flies and other insects for its continued existence, to pollinate it, and it emits a putrid, dung-and-carrion-like smell to attract them. Likewise, Dark Souls rely on the fears and the vulnerability of the other four soul groups in our cluster to help them thrive and grow.

There was an audience of about four hundred, and the place was Toronto, Canada. I was only two thirds of the way through writing *Soul Signs*, and so had no idea why I had begun to explain the five energy forces, and the subject of evil among us, but was soon to find out.

As I finished the first part of my lecture, as I often do, I asked the audience for their questions. This is usually the time when the spirit world breaks its silence and begins to give messages, and so each time someone in the audience asked a question, I would pay attention to the energy around them. And sure enough, those from the spirit world began to come through, bringing with them messages of hope, of love, of concern, and of comfort.

There was a message from a young man who had accidentally drowned. His wife and best friend, who had, since his death, married, were overjoyed to hear of his survival, and were thrilled when he told them how happy he was that they were together.

Another message was to a young woman from her mother, who had died of cancer more than five years ago. The daughter was crying and crying as she heard her mother's message. For five years she had been wracked with guilt because in her last few moments her mother had asked for water, and the doctor had not allowed it. "I should have just given her a drink," she sobbed. "I should just have given her a drink." Five years on, as I went back and forth, and through the hole, listening to the mother, saying what I saw and heard, the daughter was finally calmed and at peace with herself. "I am by a stream," said the mother, and standing with her, I watched as she bent down, cupped her hands together, and brought the crystal-clear water to her lips, and her next words made me smile. "There is enough water here for me, and I will never go thirsty again."

On and on around the room I went, taking questions, giving messages. A lot of the questions that night were about evil.

Can someone who is evil go to the light? A Dark Soul has no desire, and indeed fears light and hides from it. Their home is in the shadows.

Where do Dark Souls go when they die? When we die, we all of us go home, we return to the place of our creation.

How can you tell if a person is a Dark Soul? It is difficult to recognize a Dark Soul until they show themselves to us, or they are caught. Not all Dark Souls are clever, but cunning and slyness are two of their main traits, and so they are able to hide quite successfully behind their many guises. However, good energy has a way of recognizing evil energy, and this is where our instinctive nature plays an important role. Our feelings will tell us when things are not right. We must pay attention to and act on this instinct.

Will God accept a soul into heaven if that soul has committed evil acts? There have been many souls of light who have done or will do evil. Their reasons and excuses will vary, as will the amount of guilt or remorse they feel. Some of these souls will intentionally do harm, while for others their actions will be spontaneous. They will all, at some point, die, and will have the choice to enter the light or not. God gives them that choice. He turns no one away, no matter what their deeds, for when we step into the light we are asking God's forgiveness for our sins, both great and small.

Evil comes in many forms, I explained, and very often alluring ones. Dark Souls need victims in order to grow stronger in their evilness. Like the chameleon, they become whatever their intended victim wants them to be, slithering into a personality before they strike, like you might slip into a formfitting dress. And strike they will, again and again, never sated for more than a short while. So what can the rest of us do?

We can't stop evil unless we believe in its existence. Once we believe it, then we can fight it. With God's help, we can fight and we can win. And what weapons can we use in this battle? Right thinking and right behavior. Loving thoughts and loving actions. Tolerance, understanding, patience, caring, courage, daring, honesty. All these things, and the desire and the intention to always do the right thing—these are the weapons that will help us win.

My final example of the Sulphur sign is the story of the first time I can remember coming face-to-face with a Dark Soul. It happened many years ago, when my husband and I and some friends had gone to a nightclub, something to do with my husband's business. I had been to the restroom and was making my way slowly back to our table, occasionally stopping to watch the dancing, and it was on one of these stops that I felt it first: a kind of tugging sensation in my mind, and a strong feeling that I was being watched.

I resisted from the outset, every instinct warning of danger. Staring hard at the dance floor, I found myself making more and more of a conscious effort to resist the strange tugging sensation in my head, which was getting stronger and more difficult to ignore. I didn't want to turn around, and the more I resisted, the more sure I was that someone was watching me, trying somehow to overpower me. Soon I began to feel really hot, my head bursting with pressure, and I felt the urge to run, to find my table, back to safety. Having been used to strange energies all my life, I thought this was just another "happening"; scared and disoriented, I knew I needed to stay controlled. But feeling myself suddenly tremendously overwhelmed, I turned, and there he was, way over on the other side of the room.

The energy that came from him was overpowering and all around me. His eyes were dark and piercing, and locked firmly into mine. I tried desperately to break my gaze away and found I couldn't. At first I was frozen to the spot, and then slowly I found myself beginning to walk toward him. I couldn't stop myself—he seemed to be controlling my mind, and like metal to a magnet, I felt myself being drawn in.

His expression never changed, his eyes never left mine for a moment. One step, then two, like a sleepwalker I headed slowly toward him, and then—*bang!*—someone crashed into me, a barmaid carrying a tray of empty glasses. The tray and glasses went every which way, the girl apologized profusely, and amid the chaos my trance state was broken. Terrified, with my heart thumping in my chest, I raced as fast as I could back to my husband and friends, to safety.

But I was afraid. I had seen the face of darkness. I had felt its powerful force. And had it not been for that opportune intervention, or perhaps an angel watching over me, I cannot say if I would have been able to resist. I cannot say for sure that the stranger was a bad seed, a Dark Soul, a Dracunculus, but I clearly remember his eyes, and I even more clearly remember his energy force and how it seemed to seep into my brain, to freeze me into inaction and to render me helpless. It was a force that was being used to control.

I cannot say for sure that he was a Dark Soul, but in my heart I know that he was.

So yes, there is evil in our midst, and yes, we should be on our guard against it. But the light of God, the presence and power of our loved ones in the spirit world, and our own pure force of love will always, always win.

SO NOW YOU KNOW

Now that we are aware of the Sulphur energy group, of the Dark Soul, throughout the rest of this book we are going to address only our four primary groups and the soul signs in each. And now that you know your own group and soul sign, you know your traits, you know your flower—what now? That all depends on you. Do you see yourself in a more positive and gentle light? Well, you should. Do you realize that you have incredible potential and power? I hope so. Do you understand that you are an amazing and beautiful flower in God's garden? You surely are.

In each one of us there are negative traits—or is it just that we look at them in a negative way? Do we view them as negative because we have not been encouraged to do otherwise? Let's see.

Yes, the **Retrospective Soul** seems to have so many negative traits, but that shows us the highly sensitive nature of this soul, and the potential to give, to sympathize, to empathize with others, and also to be resilient and creative in how to turn situations around to positive and beneficial conclusions. Their innate needy behavior, as well, can be a tool that may enable them to see clearly the needs of others, which will make them a powerful ally to the underdog.

Yes, the **Dreaming Soul** can be ultrasensitive and overreact, can take the smallest thing to heart and be thoughtless at times, but we know that this reaction is not intentional and can be seen as an endearing quality, once we realize their dreaming nature means that they so often live inside their own head. This trait can strengthen their endurance of difficult or stressful situations. Not obliged to be realistic, they are able to remain ever hopeful and positive of good outcomes, and more expressive of their creative nature.

Yes, the **Bright Star Soul** can be too competitive, can tend toward drama and attention seeking, overshadowing others and getting carried away into believing that it's all about them, but it is their ego, their powerful sense of self, which will drive them to be successful in their lives and accomplish their goals. Controlling? Yes, indeed they can be, but always with the right intention, and in maturity the Bright Star is able to harness that energy into making good things happen. Too dramatic? Indeed they can be, but this trait, used wisely, can be a powerful tool to make others pay attention to important issues.

Yes, the **Hunter Soul** can be self-involved and shut out others and will sometimes, unintentionally, be exploitative and insensitive to others' needs. However, these tools will be beneficial when applied to those life situations which require single-minded and concentrated efforts in order to achieve success. Continually seeking appreciation? Certainly, but this trait gives the Hunter the ability to also appreciate and value qualities and potential in most circumstances, and even though they may not necessarily express that appreciation, nevertheless, they are able to savor life to the full.

Yes, the **Visionary Soul** can be impractical and given to flights of fancy, which can certainly cause them difficulties, especially monetary; however, these tools most definitely promote creative and expressive possibilities, leading to innovative and unique ideas. Are they prone to being negative and somewhat pessimistic about their own life situation? Yes; however, this gives us an idea of how greatly sensitive they are, which inclines them toward being more sympathetic and empathetic toward others.

Yes, the **Warrior Soul** can be can be outspoken, intimidating, head-strong, and demanding, but these traits are the tools that get them where they want to be. Exacting and rigid? Sometimes, yes, but this preciseness and the ability to stand their ground is what enables them to win battles and to achieve positive results. A hardliner? Most definitely, and when working on behalf of their community or family, their commitment to demanding right behavior of themselves and others can help them achieve incredible and often surprisingly positive results.

Yes, the **Traveler Soul** can isolate themselves, shy away from commitment, and tend to ignore emotional issues, which is not good for others, but the positive for the Traveler is that they travel light, don't carry emotional baggage, are not cluttered by conventional values, and are therefore able to see many situations from a wide perspective. They are able to take from each situation in life what they want, and what they need from this earth experience to grow in spirit.

Yes, the **Prophet Soul** can be easily taken advantage of by others, can be blind to others' negative traits, most definitely to their own detriment. In maturity, however, they may realize how important it is to give to one's own soul. Being selfless and passive, often allowing themselves to be abused, gives them a greater understanding and ability to recognize pain and hurt in others. Naive and too trusting? Yes; however, this naïveté gives them an openness that will draw others to them in friendship and love.

Yes, the **Newborn Soul** can be hard to control sometimes, but so what? Isn't this what makes them so endearing to the rest of us? And yes, they can be undiscerning and too trusting, but isn't it better to be that way than not to trust at all? And boy, how frustrating it can be that they are a little slow sometimes to grasp situations, but isn't that the negative perception of those who are impatient, in contrast to than the wonderful naïveté that allows our Newborn to be so open and willing to accept others for who they are?

Yes, the **Seeker Soul** can be blinded by intellect, dispassionate, and detached, but surely those traits can be used positively and are great tools in assessing situations calmly and unemotionally. Indeed, the Seeker can be critical of others, but used positively and with real thought, that criticism can be constructive and helpful. Definitely the inability to express emotion can be a problem, but recognizing this trait, and overcoming it, can make them that much more sympathetic and empathetic.

Yes, the **Peacemaker Soul** can most definitely be selfless to the point of self-damage, and they will suffer for this, and in this suffering will inevitably understand and be more sensitive to the suffering of others. This ability to empathize is one of the most endearing qualities of this soul. Quietly judgmental? Yes, and will judge by their own set of standards, which will be raised again and again because of this. As long as this practice is not taken to the extreme, the Peacemaker can use this tool to stretch themselves.

Yes, the **Old Soul** can most definitely be a creature of habit, can be frozen into inaction by a need to do the right thing and often tries to be all things to all people; but can always be relied upon, stalwart and dependable. Having high standards and being demanding of right behavior makes this soul sometimes tough to be around, but those high standards will provide a benchmark, an incentive, an inspiration for all those connected to this soul to reach higher goals. Their tendency to control, in maturity, will be directed toward themselves, and taking more control of their own lives can only be enriching and fulfilling.

In each one of us there are traits which, if not exercised wisely, can lead us astray and can stunt our spiritual growth and limit our spiritual destiny. We often learn by example how to be or how not to be, and we need to take responsibility for knowing better.

When God placed us on this planet, He gave us life, He gave us opportunity, and He gave us gifts. Many gifts. He gave us tools to enable us, to help us get the best from our earth experience. He gave us power. He gave us strength. All these gifts, all these insights, all this power—and all of it ours. Ours to use.

I am so grateful.

PART·FOUR

RELATIONSHIPS

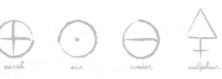

fire   *earth*   *air*   *water*   *sulphur*

PLAYMATES, HELPMATES, SOUL MATES

Since the beginning of time, man . . . and woman . . . has looked for a suitable mate. Back then, the primary reason for getting together was procreation, the need to ensure the future of our human species. Of course, that is no longer a concern, as there are enough of us on this planet for our race to continue its existence at least until someone blows us all up. And that isn't going to happen for quite a while yet.

So, our reasons for wanting a relationship have changed, and now most of us look for a soul mate, *our* soul mate, that one person who will make all our dreams come true and make us happy for the rest of our lives.

Love is in the air, or so the song goes. So too the movies and thousands of romance novels—they all tell us that true love is ours, just waiting around the corner, and some of us, the lucky ones, will find it. Now if this is true, that we all do have a soul mate out there somewhere, why are they so elusive? The percentage of happy and contented relationships is low and getting lower by the decade. If we are to believe that each soul has its ideal mate as its destiny, I for one want to know what happened to mine!

John, I seem to remember, was my very first soul mate, and he truly was pretty wonderful. He was a Water sign, and was also from the same Extrovert energy source as I, an Old Soul. In fact, we were a perfect match. Of course, I was young, too young, only sixteen, and my father disapproved, so the relationship was doomed.

Then there was Andrew, my first serious adult soul mate. It was love at first sight. This was it, my heart sang out. I was so blinded by love, though, that I had no idea my soul mate already had a mate, that he was married. There was no doubt that Andrew was in love with me, as I was with him. There was no doubt that our relationship was meant to be— just not forever.

There was another kind of love song I was singing after Andrew, about broken hearts and love not meant to be. My life was in pieces, and I told myself that my quest for true love was over. I was not looking anymore. This love stuff was too painful. And I began to be happy in my solitude, really happy, burying my dreams and my hopes in my work. And it worked. I no longer hurt, I no longer cried, and for the first time in my life I discovered *me* and became truly content. I became my own soul mate, my own friend, able to fulfill all my important needs. But, then, you know what they say: When you stop looking, love looks for you.

Is your soul mate out there somewhere? For me there were at least a couple more mistakes waiting to be made. Or were these "mistakes" simply opportunities waiting to happen?

Grey Eagle tells me that there are three kinds of soul mates. There are those souls who are meant to come into our lives for the purpose of growth and learning, having decided before birth that this would be part of their earth-life experience. These souls are our helpmates, and are not necessarily romantic partners, although they can be. Other helpmates are our parents, our siblings, our friends, our children, and even those brief encounters that we sometimes have . . . when one soul touches the heart and soul of another, as happened to me just the other day when a five-year-old boy was introduced to me. In his shyness, he at first averted his eyes, but then turned, looked up at me from under his eyelashes, and gave me a knowing, sweet smile. That tiny smile, that knowing, connected with my soul and helped me confirm that my life was in place, and as it should be.

Playmates are also a type of soul mate. I use the term to describe those people we meet whom we connect to, have things in common with. They may in fact share our same energy and come out of the same pocket, but their influence on our growth process might be minimal, and noticeable only through the good experiences that we have. Still, in this role, when they touch even a small part of our spirit, they become important in the greater plan. We remember them. Our soul remembers them. I had a friend, Ann, who was definitely a playmate; chatting with her, having coffee, going shopping, meeting once a week for dinner really helped me at a time when my marriage was a disaster and I needed a friend . . . a playmate. Someone to talk to and hang out with. It eased my loneliness tremendously.

Then, of course, there is that person most of us think of as a soul mate: that one soul who is out there somewhere searching for us, even as we, often subconsciously, search for them; that soul who, when joined with us, will make us complete. Happiness, contentment, true love, boundless connectedness—we believe our soul mate will deliver all of this and more, and make our dream come true.

In all of the relationships we've ever had, whether with playmates, help-mates, or soul mates, there have been good reasons why we have been drawn to certain other souls, and good reasons why we are now apart. For those of you who have found your soul mate, your happy marriage, your fulfilled relationship, the reasons are clear: You are with a soul whose energy flow and soul sign is compatible with yours, and you were both mature enough to realize it. Not only were you meant to meet, you both had the right attitude and the maturity to work on and fix all those things in your relationship that were difficult.

Had I met John, or should I meet him at some future time, both of us more mature and worldly wise, the chances of a truly fulfilled and happy relationship are very high. Of course, when I say John, what I really mean is a Water sign, an Old Soul, who would be my most compatible mate and my best chance at happiness. This would be my soul mate.

Once you understand how different soul signs interact, you can see why some relationships do not work out no matter how hard you both try. It is simply a clash of energy, of two incompatible soul signs. No one's fault, not theirs, not yours. You are both just acting in character, driven by your own particular energy force. Each of us has the possibility of a good match, but we have to learn which soul signs are right for us and which are not. Then, of course, we have to have the wisdom and the maturity to know when to hold on and when to let go.

Of all the soul signs, the four who are most capable of bringing balance to a relationship are our Central soul signs: the Dreaming Soul, the Visionary Soul, the Prophet Soul, and the Peacemaker Soul. If you are an extreme energy sign, which is any one of the other eight signs in the soul cluster, and you are in a relationship with a Central and balanced sign, then your chances of a good relationship have improved dramatically.

Relationships between two Extrovert signs or two Introvert signs can be really good or really bad. Because both are moving in the same direction, there will be a great understanding of how and why each partner ticks. However, there will also be times of power struggles, particularly between Fire signs and Earth signs, the two more obvious and obviously powerful energy sources, and this will create inevitable conflicts. The most dangerous, and perhaps the most difficult combination of signs, is between extreme Extroverts and extreme Introverts. Total opposites, they are often fatally attracted, but their energies will cause great clashes.

I have friends, a couple who are very dear to me. She is a Seeker Soul and he is a Newborn Soul, and although Water signs and Air signs are generally compatible, these two signs are the least compatible combination of these two groups. Why? One has an Introvert energy flow and the other an Extrovert energy flow. They are both reasonable people who hate conflict, but because their energy flows in opposite directions, they will clash, they do clash, and even though they clash less and less often as they mature and have a better understanding of each other, when they do clash . . . watch out. The fallout is not pleasant.

Extremes can get along really well as friends, but in romantic or more personal relationships, such as mother–daughter, father–son, husband–wife, business partner–business partner, employer–employee, in these relationships, Introvert and Extrovert soul signs are likely to clash. There are, of course, exceptions. There are some souls who have reached a level of maturity and growth where they can, and do, make it work. Still, even with real maturity, personal relationships with two people who have opposite and extreme energy sources, especially if they are in the same soul group, will inevitably have serious and often unresolved clashes.

Thinking of all the couples I know who are and who are not compatible, it is easy for me to see why some relationships work and why some don't. Let's look at a few of these relationships together and see what we learn.

Sally is a Visionary Soul, an Earth sign; David is a Traveler Soul, an Air sign. They have been dating for almost two years, and the relationship for the most part is good. David is generally passive and easygoing, true to his Traveler traits, and shows a reluctance to fully commit. In his late forties, he has never married or lived with anyone, and he finds it hard to take that next step.

For the Traveler, loving someone may just not be enough reason to settle down. He is always afraid that if he takes a step in one direction, then he might miss something better elsewhere.

Sally, the Visionary, is also true to her soul type. She has a real need to belong, to feel protected and nurtured by her mate, and feels somewhat vulnerable in the no-man's-land her mate has put her in. If she is patient and waits, her patience might pay off—or not.

David, the Traveler, will not be pushed, as far as relationships go, and has a need to stay very much in control. If nagged or bullied, he could be driven, by his flow of energy, to act. If she wants this relationship to work, Sally should concentrate on how to be patient rather than trying to force her mate into making a decision.

If David does make a decision to move in, to commit, Sally has to make him feel no pressure from her whatsoever. As long as Sally allows David to take his own actions instead of taking actions for them both, which Earth signs can have a tendency to do, they have a good chance. However, David also has to understand Sally's need for reassurance—one of the Visionary's main needs.

They seem compatible, so what makes it so? Simple. David is an extreme Introvert energy, and Sally is a balanced Central energy. There is very little push and pull, as their energy will often flow the same way. Their clashes, although inevitable, as in all relationships, will be few and will happen only when Sally's energy flow moves toward an Extrovert energy stream, when she will seem to go against David in some things. This ability to move back and forth, or to stay centered, is the nature of all the Central soul signs and has its distinct advantages in all circumstances.

Debbie, a Fire sign, a Dreaming Soul, is with Reg, a Retrospective Soul. Both are Fire signs. How will this work? Married for twenty-eight years, and not without many trials, as you would expect from two souls with such a strong driving energy force, the relationship is nevertheless well and truly cemented.

Reg, true to his Retrospective's character traits, is rarely satisfied, and a big complainer. No matter how good life is for him, and his life is very good, it never seems like it's enough. Always with his glass half empty, never half full, he struggles with his need for perfection. Our Retrospective Soul, if you remember, has the hardest time perhaps of all the soul signs, and his negative nature is difficult to live with. What soul sign, then, could possibly be compatible?

Dreaming Souls have some really wonderful character traits. Debbie uses her driving energy force in a seemingly quiet and unassuming way; you would never guess at the iron will and passionate nature underneath that seemingly passive persona. The fact that she and Reg are from the same source, the same pocket of energy, means that they instinctively know each other very well. More important, the ability of the Dreaming Soul to see things through rose-colored glasses is what makes this relationship compatible. Debbie is able to see her man as that knight in shining armor. She sees past his negativity, she understands his need for perfection, and she firmly holds on to her dream. Consequently, for the most part, she is quite content with what she has. Reg, the Retrospective, is as happy as he will admit to being—truly a Retrospective Soul.

Their marriage works. Reg is an extreme Introvert energy, and Debbie is a balanced Central energy, able to flow with her husband's energy quite easily, just as Sally and David do, which means few real clashes, very little pull and push, and real harmony.

A few more: Gordon is a Hunter; Sandra is a Warrior. Both Earth signs, this couple was drawn to each other from the beginning—like attracts like. But their energy flows in opposite directions, which makes them almost completely incompatible. What was good about this relationship, and what would, under circumstances other than romantic, have produced a strong friendship, is that each has an energy that the other admires and understands. The Warrior Soul, drawn to the Hunter because all Warriors need strength and support from those around them, instinctively knew the Hunter's power, his strength. The Hunter, drawn to Sandra like a magnet for similar reasons, saw someone who was not needy or demanding of attention he subconsciously knew he could not, and did not want to, give. Both so alike, but poles apart. As their energy flowed so obviously in opposite directions, their relationship could not sustain the power struggle. Clash, clash, clash.

An example of two Water signs is Denise, an Old Soul, and Michael, a Peacemaker, who have been happily married for twenty-seven years. One is an extreme Extrovert sign, one a Central sign. The Peacemaker perfectly complements the Old Soul, as they come from the same source, the same flow. Each is able to evaluate and compromise in all areas of their life together. Even though they have their arguments, as every couple does, Michael and Denise have a well-balanced energy flow, which produces peace and harmony in their ideal relationship.

Joan, a Bright Star, and Steve, a Traveler, both have that extreme energy flow, one Extrovert, one Introvert. One—exciting, high energy, playful, needing the limelight and demanding attention, a Fire sign. The other—an Air sign, easygoing, mostly passive, enjoys his partner's obvious differences. Having many of the same interests, they seemed quite compatible, and their relationship lasted for several years, in part due to the fact that they only saw each other two or three times a week and didn't live together. Then one day, Joan realized she needed more than a part-time relationship. This was the beginning of the end. And so began those clashes, those inevitable power clashes that occur between Extrovert and Introvert energies. Steve, the Traveler, was generally easygoing and loved the excitement and thrill that the Bright Star brought into his life, but he could not commit. The Bright Star needed her emotional security. She needed to know she was number one in his life, but he just couldn't do it. His Introvert energy was concentrated on what was best for him. This is an example of two extreme forces of energy, one flowing north, one flowing south, creating an imbalance of energy. The inevitable happens: They clash, big time, and . . . the end.

In relationships, clashes come mainly when we try to change another person, or when we wish a person could be different—when the imbalance becomes noticeable by another person's behavior, and we view that behavior as bad or inappropriate. But we know now that there are some things we just cannot change. What if we could simply see that person as a Bright Star, not meaning to be insensitive to others but simply driven by their energy force, Fire? What if we could judge a person not so much as "controlling" but rather as having a need to make a plan, driven by their energy force, Earth? Or how about that Air sign, saying nothing and accepting their fate when you dearly wish they would speak up? And what of those compromisers who drive you crazy because they overevaluate an issue to the point that you just want to say, "Make up your mind!"? Understanding and accepting that they are Water signs, seeing them merely as acting in character, can make your relationship more harmonious.

Of course, this is easier said than done. Another example of two people having opposite energy flow is my own marriage, to a Traveler, an extreme Introvert energy, while my energy is Extrovert. We were married for fifteen years, and many of those years were good, probably due to the fact that he was an easygoing Air sign and I am an Earth sign naturally inclined to be hopeful. He was so easygoing that bills were never paid, and marriage vows were never kept. There was a long line of mistresses, but hey, as long as the wife (that was me) never found out! My husband, as most Travelers are, was a really nice but immature soul. I, on the other hand, also immature, could be bossy and demanding, intuitively knowing what was going on, always hoping I was wrong. Had he not played around, had I been less demanding, had we both worked on those less-than-nice character traits, we may well still be together, and for the most part, at least content, even if not ecstatically happy. Oh, for those "if onlys."

Now I know better, and if there is ever another opportunity out there for me, another chance at a relationship, the first thing I will do is figure out his soul sign and make sure that our signs are compatible . . . and if they are not, you can bet I'll be running, very fast, in the other direction!

If you are already in a relationship that is strained, already clashing, the hurdles you face in fixing things can seem insurmountable. But they might be overcome. As you figure out your own soul sign and the soul sign of your partner, it is easier to see your respective strengths and weaknesses. Once you understand your actions and interactions, you may figure out where to make adjustments. When you know your soul sign, it becomes easier to make sound judgments and decisions about the kind of partnership you want; once you know what you need, you stand a greater chance of finding it. And you can prevent disastrous relationships by avoiding those obviously incompatible soul signs. Prevention, as they say, is better than cure.

All relationships, no matter what combination of soul signs they are, can be very much a balancing act, as we all know. And in our modern world, the world of working couples, the balance of energy seems to be all over the place, and it is much harder to define what each person's role is in the relationship.

Our spirit's energy flowing through us reveals its imbalance in our mood swings. In a comfortable, safe, and happy environment, our soul's energy flow will be balanced. Meditation, yoga, or exercise can help bring us into balance; so can good relationships, healthy working environments, a balanced diet, and emotional stability. Finding things in life that bring us balance can only be a good thing. Knowing what the needs of our soul are, and how important it is to recognize our energy source, our soul sign, is the first major step. Finding the right balance, learning as much as we can of our soul's needs, and the needs of our mate—these are ways to ensure our happiness.

So, finally, we have the key. We don't have to take unnecessary chances. We don't have to make the same mistakes over and over again. Our sons and daughters don't have to make hard choices, or wonder what their chances of divorce or loneliness will be. The game of love is no longer hit-or-miss, a shot in the dark, that frightening gamble we have often been compelled to take. No longer is love a game of chance.

Life is a juggling act, relationships take work, and however we do it, and no matter how successfully, most of us manage a reasonable balance in our lives. We may make up for the imbalance of our personal relationships by putting our energy into other areas. Throwing ourselves into our family or our work, we find compatible people to be around who make us feel good. We find like souls we can relate to and share our lives with, who fulfill our needs as we fulfill theirs.

Life is hard for most of us, and made more difficult by confused communications and misunderstandings, which happen all the time. The exciting thing about soul signs is that we can use our new knowledge to unlock many closed doors, and to avoid confusion and misunderstandings. We have been given the opportunity to finally "get it," to understand ourselves and to understand others.

CONNECTING THE DOTS

So which soul signs go best together? What energy group is our soul mate most likely to come from? To know the answers to these questions, we must understand how our elemental energies interact with one another. To know how or even if we'll get along with someone, we need to look closely at these elemental forces to divine their needs and their gifts.

For example, if you are a Fire sign, your most compatible group is Air.

If you are an Earth sign, your most compatible group is Water.

Fire signs and Earth signs need to be fed. Air signs and Water signs do not have that same need, and are more able to feed themselves.

Why? How does it work? In our first case, it is important to know that without air, fire cannot exist. And, in our second case, without water the earth becomes barren, dry, and cracked, and turns to dust. In an ideal world, then, when we are looking for our most perfect soul mate, we are looking for one which can feed us or which we can feed, so it is helpful to consider that Fire *needs* Air, and Earth *needs* Water. This is where we start.

It is also instructive to remember that for an Extrovert energy, the most compatible mate would be either an Extrovert or Central energy. For an Introvert energy, the most compatible mate would be either another Introvert, or a Central, balanced energy. Energies that naturally flow the same way, or are capable of flowing the same way, result in less conflict, less aggravation, and fewer misunderstandings—important factors in any relationship.

Fire signs need to be paid attention to. They need accolades, emotional nurturing, and awareness from others of their highly sensitive nature.

Earth signs require participation. They need to interact with others, otherwise their planning and strategizing natures are unfulfilled.

Air signs float. They need space, a certain amount of freedom, and although they love to be with others, they are more than capable of doing their own thing.

Water signs also need space, space to flow, to channel their energy. They have an independent, free-flowing spirit, even though others may well depend on them.

In a perfect world, this is what your perfect soul mate would be:

YOUR SIGN		YOUR IDEAL MATE'S SIGN
FIRE ○	**Retrospective**	*Traveler Soul or Prophet Soul*
	Dreaming	*Newborn Soul, Prophet Soul, or Traveler Soul*
	Bright Star	*Newborn Soul or Prophet Soul*
EARTH ⊕	**Hunter**	*Seeker Soul or Peacemaker Soul*
	Visionary	*Old Soul, Peacemaker Soul, or Seeker Soul*
	Warrior	*Old Soul or Peacemaker Soul*
AIR ⊙	**Traveler**	*Retrospective Soul or Dreaming Soul*
	Prophet	*Bright Star Soul, Dreaming Soul, or Retrospective Soul*
	Newborn	*Bright Star Soul or Dreaming Soul*
WATER ⊖	**Seeker**	*Hunter Soul or Visionary Soul*
	Peacemaker	*Warrior Soul, Visionary Soul, or Hunter Soul*
	Old	*Warrior Soul or Visionary Soul*

This ideal combination of soul signs is what best connects the dots, is what best feeds us and gives us light. However, there are other combinations that also work well together and give us a good chance of happiness.

We know that our Central soul signs have the best chance of finding a compatible relationship because they are capable of going with the flow and are therefore more easily able to combine their energy with another soul's, without the excessive friction that our Extrovert and Introvert signs would have. Our Air signs and Water signs are also compatible. Balanced, free-flowing, they are more able to nourish themselves than our Fire and Earth signs can. Air floats over water. Water flows beneath air. These signs work well together without necessarily interacting. Neither has a need of the other, but each is capable of complementing the other's energy flow without taking away from it.

Let's look at each soul sign and see how and why they get along with others.

FIRE	Retrospective	Traveler Soul or Prophet Soul
	Dreaming	Newborn Soul, Prophet Soul, or Traveler Soul
	Bright Star	Newborn Soul or Prophet Soul

The Retrospective Soul

Our Retrospective Soul, as we have discovered, needs perfection, needs attention, and needs a mate who can deal with their ultrasensitive nature.

Emotional, and often starved of that oxygen they so need, they need air, but not in a gusting or forceful way. The Prophet Soul, calm and uncomplicated, able to accept most people, is least affected adversely by the complex and sometimes difficult and demanding nature of the Retrospective Soul.

What the Retrospective Soul does not need is to be criticized, to be harshly judged, to be told what to do or how to think. What the Retrospective Soul does not need is for their mate to fan the flame to the point where the fire combusts, explodes to the point of self-damage. A Bright Star and Warrior Soul are the Retrospective Soul's most dangerous combination, and will create the most damaging and emotionally disturbing partnership.

The Dreaming Soul

Our Dreaming Soul needs to be appreciated, but unlike the Bright Star, an Extrovert energy, the Dreaming Soul's needs are much less obvious. Their flame, as with all Fire signs, needs to be fanned, but in a more subtle and un-obtrusive way. All the Air signs will get along well with the Dreaming Soul, as they give oxygen, nourishment, and encouragement, and encouragement is what our Dreaming Soul craves most. Perhaps surprisingly, the Retrospective Soul can also work, but can also be dangerous if the Dreaming Soul's rose-colored glasses come off and they see their mate as he or she really is, instead of who they dream they are.

What the Dreaming Soul does not need, as with all Fire signs, is to be ignored, to have their sensitive nature abused, to be forced to face those "realities" that others may have to live with. What the Dreaming Soul does not need is for their mate to dull the flame to the point where their fire becomes dampened, to the point where their dreams are dashed and they become uncertain of their own self-worth. A Bright Star, Retrospective, Warrior, or Hunter Soul are the Dreaming Soul's most dangerous combinations, as they are the most overtly forceful of all the soul signs and can tend, in immaturity, to be too centered on their own goals. However, as a Central and balanced energy force, the Dreaming Soul can, with effort and understanding, make even those relationships work, to a point.

The Bright Star Soul

Our Bright Star needs to shine, to be the center of attention, to be admired. In other words, their flame, their energy always needs to be fanned, to be given oxygen, to be kept alive. Newborn Souls are able to do this really well, as they are open and out there and love to be excited by the Bright Star's ability to sparkle at their innovative and sometimes naive and eccentric ideas.

What the Bright Star does not need is to be ignored, put down, or unappreciated, or to be told that they are too sensitive, too emotional, or out of control. What the Bright Star does not need is for their mate to fan the flame to the point where the fire gets out of control. The Retrospective Soul and the Hunter Soul are the Bright Star's most dangerous combinations—unless, through learned behavior or extreme and dysfunctional upbringings, the Bright Star has learned to love/hate the continual and constant battles that this combination of energies inevitably brings.

EARTH 	Hunter	Seeker Soul or Peacemaker Soul
	Visionary	Old Soul, Peacemaker Soul, or Seeker Soul
	Warrior	Old Soul or Peacemaker Soul

The Hunter Soul

The Hunter Soul needs to have a goal, something to aim for, a place to reach. Single-minded, they need a place, a situation, a lifestyle which allows them to concentrate their efforts on whatever project or plan they have. Seeker Souls are able to feed the Hunter's insatiable desire for new ideas, new goals, new aims, as they themselves are always searching for new information, and have the ability to be constructively critical, which is the kind of interaction both soul signs need.

What the Hunter Soul does not need is a lack of control, opposition to their plans, or interference with their aims and goals. The Hunter does not need a mate who is highly sensitive, who needs attention and continued reassurance of love and affection, or whose energy is so overtly powerful as to seem threatening. The Warrior and Bright Star Souls are the Hunter's most dangerous combinations, as they are the most overtly Extrovert energies and are seen by the Hunter as threatening to the Hunter's need to have control. These combinations will result in much conflict, frustration, and angst.

The Visionary Soul

The Visionary Soul needs to express their ability to create an environment that gives them the best home life and that suits their social life. They need to share their insights, their ability to sense and to be sensitive toward others, and they need to express their uniqueness. Needing involvement with others, just as all Earth signs do, their well must be replenished and never allowed to run dry. Nourishment needs to come in the form of encouragement, a sense of being valued, and a positive reaction to their unique capabilities. All the Water signs will work well, as they nourish Earth signs.

What the Visionary Soul does not need is to have their hopes and strategies criticized. What the Visionary does not need is a mate whose own plans become so much more important that they override and cause the Visionary to question their own fragile sense of self-worth. Bright Star or Retrospective Souls are the Visionary Soul's most dangerous combinations; both Fire signs, they are easily able to consume, to burn out the Visionary Soul's empathetic and sensitive nature.

The Warrior Soul

The Warrior Soul needs to have a cause, no matter how small that cause may be. They need a plan, a strategy, which could be as simple as being a volunteer committee member on the local school board, or as ambitious as political expert of the year. They need to protect and serve and always to act. Old Souls are able to replenish this energy really well, as they are reasoned and full of common sense, able to flow and to nourish with their innate sense of groundedness.

What the Warrior Soul does not need is high drama, insensitive actions, or continual opposition. The Warrior does not need their mate to be so opposing that they are sucked dry by a continual battle of wills. Retrospective and Hunter Souls are the Warrior's most dangerous combinations, as they are both overtly powerful like the Warrior, and they are both Introvert signs, energy that directly opposes that of the Warrior Soul. These combinations are likely to be destructive.

AIR		
Traveler	*Retrospective Soul or Dreaming Soul*	
Prophet	*Bright Star Soul, Dreaming Soul, or Retrospective Soul*	
Newborn	*Bright Star Soul or Dreaming Soul*	

The Traveler Soul

Our Traveler Soul needs freedom to roam, either physically, emotionally, or imaginatively. Once again, like all Air signs, they are not demanding or pushy, but rather more casual and easygoing. They need calm, fun, excitement, an uncluttered environment both at home and at work, and an easy life with as few responsibilities as they can get away with. Dreaming Souls are able to give all this, allowing the Traveler to get what they need without compromising themselves in any way.

What the Traveler Soul does not need is forced responsibilities and a limiting home life. Travelers do not need a mate who is disciplined, regimented, and strategizing, who is headstrong and demanding, who has a tendency to take on others' problems and issues and bring them home, disrupting that quiet and peaceful space, intruding on the Traveler's need for a quiet life. The Warrior Soul is the Traveler's most dangerous combination; one Introvert, one Extrovert, these opposing forces are bound to create feelings of pure frustration and irritation—bad for both signs.

The Prophet Soul

The Prophet needs to be needed, to be useful, helpful. They need space, as do all Air signs, and this might come in the form of outdoor activity or in a nonstressful and stimulating work environment. Caring and sharing is what brings light to the Prophet Soul. As a Central and balanced energy force, the Prophet can find a place in most environments; however, fun loving and with a great sense of humor, the Bright Star gives them the light they need to shine, without having to be center stage, happy to bask in another's sunshine.

What the Prophet Soul does not need is to have their generous nature abused or taken for granted. The Prophet does not need a mate who under-values them, who dismisses or cuts them out of conversations or situations, who excludes them in some way. Again, as a Central and balanced energy, the Prophet is able, with some effort, to make most relationships work. The Hunter Soul is the Prophet Soul's most dangerous combination, as, unin-tentionally, they will often override, manipulate, use, and take for granted all that is special and gentle and kind about the Prophet.

The Newborn Soul

Our Newborn Soul needs to be stimulated by new things, by original thinking and innovative ideas. They need to be involved, yet they need air, space in which to express themselves, to be creative, whether as a cook, a homemaker, an inventor, or in selling something new. They need to be al-lowed to be themselves. The Bright Star is a good match, as they are bright and shiny as a new toy, and they make things happen—fun things, new things—and they are able to fascinate, and to shine.

What the Newborn Soul does not need is to be ridiculed. The Newborn does not need a mate who puts them down, who finds their naïveté a nega-tive as opposed to a positive, who continually tells them to grow up, or who is generally negative or depressed. Retrospective and Hunter Souls are the Newborn Soul's most dangerous combinations; both Introvert energies, the absolute opposite of the Newborn, they will oppose and frustrate, causing confusion, hurt, and a feeling of utter uselessness.

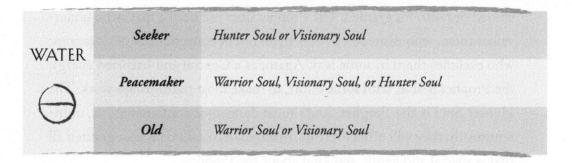

WATER	Seeker	Hunter Soul or Visionary Soul
	Peacemaker	Warrior Soul, Visionary Soul, or Hunter Soul
	Old	Warrior Soul or Visionary Soul

The Seeker Soul

The Seeker needs complex stimulation. They need to be intellectually stretched and challenged, to stay unemotional in emotional situations. Like all Water signs, they need to be able to flow, with as few restrictions as possible, with the freedom to move, to explore, to seek at their own desired pace. Hunter Souls, who have the same energy flow, bring intriguing and exciting situations, are involved in their own goals, and act as the perfect channel for this Water sign.

What the Seeker Soul does not need is to be intellectually stifled, bored, or hampered in their searching. The Seeker does not need a mate who tries to harness their energy, to control or dictate or distract, a mate whose emotional needs, attention seeking, and neediness suck them dry. A Bright Star Soul is the Seeker Soul's most dangerous combination, and will cause overflow, a tidal reaction, and a continuous battle for both signs.

The Peacemaker Soul

The Peacemaker Soul needs to nurture, to feed, to be a mediator, to be needed. They need family or family substitutes, such as coworkers or friendships that require interdependence. They need to empathize, to be the go-between, the solver of problems and arguments, the arbitrator; to give advice and have that advice taken seriously and valued; to be involved. As a Water sign, and a Central and balanced energy force, all Earth signs get along well; however, the Warrior, needing interaction, and involved with others themselves, always having a cause, will bring fulfillment and a sense of real value.

What the Peacemaker Soul does not need is to be ignored, underrated, or undervalued. The Peacemaker does not need a mate who does not, or cannot, interact on an emotional level, or a spouse who is never there, involved in projects outside the family to the extent that family life is diminished or damaged. A Retrospective Soul is the most dangerous combination, as without meaning to, they will push our Peacemaker to the limits of their patience and tolerance.

The Old Soul

The Old Soul needs to have interaction without restriction; opportunities for great social gatherings, usually orchestrated by themselves; and alone time, that private "me" time. They need ebb and flow, involvement when they feel like it, and they need to be listened to, valued, taken seriously, and to have fun. Dependable and grounded, they need to be depended upon. Warrior Souls are able to value their great reasoning skills, their ability to compromise, their sense of fair play, and their need for justice and doing the right thing.

What the Old Soul does not need is insensitive or cruel behavior, rudeness, or aggression. The Old Soul does not need a mate who drives forward with their own needs, their own expression, without considering the needs of others. Retrospective and Hunter Souls are the Old Soul's most dangerous combinations—both Introvert energies, looking first to their own needs, then to the needs of others, in direct contrast to the Old Soul's energy flow. These combinations lead to great misunderstandings about the need for selfishness, which causes friction.

Now we better understand our interactions with others, which is particularly helpful when considering a romantic relationship. We know who our most compatible and least compatible life partners might be. In all likelihood, if you fall in love with your perfect soul match, then you are likely to stay in love, to grow old together happily; any serious problems or disagreements will be dealt with in positive ways. Of course, no relationship, no matter how ideal, will be guaranteed argument free, but by knowing the sign of our ideal soul mate, we greatly increase our chances for a lifelong and fulfilling partnership.

Likewise, if you fall in love with your most dangerous soul match, then you may struggle with love. Serious problems or disagreements might be dealt with in negative ways. With a partner whose energy is always pulling in the opposite direction, the chances for a harmonious partnership are greatly diminished.

These are the best and the worst combinations, but we don't live in an ideal world, and the truth is that most of us, in fact all of us, are imperfect. Do we want the perfect mate? Of course we do. But life is meant to help our growth, to give us opportunities to learn about ourselves—and about other imperfect human beings. Many of us will fall for someone other than our best or worst soul matches. These relationships might not be perfect, yet they can still be beautiful.

OUR WIDER POSSIBILITIES

Now that we've seen what soul sign we'd be best with, and why, it might be disappointing or even depressing to consider that the person we are involved with, whether a spouse or a significant other, is not that sign. Does this mean that the relationship is doomed? Absolutely not. We all have a number of possibly compatible soul mates, it's just that some of them may require more tolerance, more understanding, more give-and-take than others.

As we've learned, the biggest indicator of compatibility is energy flow. Same or similar flows, such as External–External or External–Central, are likely to get along, while opposite flows, such as External–Internal, are not. Opposites may attract, but when looking for your forever soul mate, go with the flow.

Because we don't always end up with our most desirable or our least desirable (thank goodness) soul sign, but someone somewhere in between, let's take a look at our wider possibilities for a soul mate: the signs we're most likely to end up with. It's also helpful to consider the following when looking for playmates and helpmates.

Below you will see how each soul sign, while maybe not technically the best (or worst) choice for a mate, will react to and interact with the energy of the others, so that we know where we stand, if and when we get involved. Since it is energy flow that influences our attraction to others and determines our compatibility, we'll start with the signs that flow with extreme energies, Extrovert and Introvert, and then look at the signs in our balanced, less obvious Central-energy group. For each soul sign, the first two potential soul mates are your best bets, your best choices, and in that order, while the next five or six choices are more or less attractive as mates. Read on, and see for yourself.

ENERGY GROUP		INTROVERT	CENTRAL	EXTROVERT
◯	FIRE	Retrospective	Dreaming	Bright Star
⊕	EARTH	Hunter	Visionary	Warrior
☉	AIR	Traveler	Prophet	Newborn
⊖	WATER	Seeker	Peacemaker	Old
♀	SULPHUR	Dark	Dark	Dark

Bright Star Soul

The **Newborn Soul** will make the Bright Star feel stimulated and admired, and the Bright Star will love the Newborn's innovative ideas and openness.

The Bright Star will respond to the sensitivity and nurturing nature of the **Prophet Soul**, and will be warmed by those traits.

With the **Warrior Soul** there will be power struggles and control issues, and the Bright Star will sometimes feel put to one side, left behind, even unloved.

The Bright Star will tend to ignore the advice of the **Old Soul** and will tend to underestimate them and be insensitive to their needs.

When interacting with a **Dreaming Soul**, the Bright Star can become irritated, controlling, and a little overpowering, if not careful.

With the **Visionary Soul** there will be definite control issues, as the Bright Star can underestimate that sign's strength and ignore their needs.

The Bright Star tends to manipulate and abuse the compromising nature of the **Peacemaker Soul**.

The Warrior Soul

The Warrior and the **Old Soul** are a perfect combination, as the Warrior will love the reasoning and evaluating traits of their partner.

The Warrior responds well to reason and compromise, and loves the **Peacemaker Soul**'s groundedness.

The Warrior will not respond well to the **Bright Star Soul**'s continual need for attention and reassurance.

The Warrior will be irritated by the **Newborn Soul**'s undisciplined nature and their inability to plan and to strategize.

The Warrior will be too demanding of the **Dreaming Soul,** and might expect impossible behavior, such as wanting the Dreaming Soul to reason and use common sense.

There's a danger that the Warrior might underestimate the **Visionary Soul**'s strength of character, and there will definitely be some control issues at times.

If not careful, the Warrior can take advantage of the **Prophet Soul**'s easygoing attitude and will tend to use and even sometimes abuse their giving and passive nature.

The Newborn Soul

The Newborn will be excited and inspired by the **Bright Star Soul**—a really good match.

The Newborn and the **Dreaming Soul**, Air and Fire, will have few clashes, but this might cause both to stray into nonaction, which can be both good and bad.

The Newborn and the **Prophet Soul** is a combination that might be a little too passive at times for both partners, but it will certainly be a peaceful and calm relationship.

If not careful, the Newborn might be tempted to take advantage of the **Peacemaker Soul**'s compromising nature to get their own way too often.

The Newborn may not react well to the control issues and might feel somewhat intimidated and restrained by the **Visionary Soul**.

The Newborn will struggle with those often restraining traits of the **Warrior Soul**, and might feel there is too much planning and strategizing in the relationship and not enough freedom to be themselves.

With an **Old Soul**, there no doubt will sometimes be a little too much restraining, from the Newborn Soul's point of view, which might irritate them and cause them stress.

The Old Soul

The Old Soul and the **Warrior Soul** are a perfect combination—both reasoning, both grounded—and the Old Soul will react well to the Warrior's action-taking nature.

The Old Soul can be irritated sometimes by the **Visionary Soul**'s need to be continually reassured, but both have the desire to listen and be listened to.

The **Peacemaker Soul** has the same flow, but the Old Soul could become bored if there is not enough intrigue or diversity in the relationship.

The **Prophet Soul** might be a little too passive, and the Old Soul could become bored.

The Old Soul might get irritated and impatient with the **Dreaming Soul**'s unrealistic traits.

The Old Soul would definitely control a partnership with a **Newborn Soul**, but usually in a positive way, trying to use sensitivity and caring to do the right thing for both of them.

There will be way too much spark in the **Bright Star Soul** for the Old Soul, and there's a definite danger of flooding, as irritation and impatience take hold of them both.

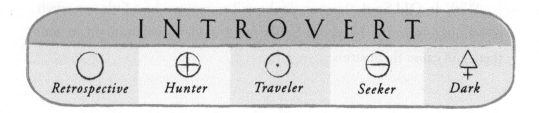

The Retrospective Soul

The Retrospective Soul will be responsive to and intrigued by the **Traveler Soul**, who will have a calming and settling effect on them, discouraging arguments.

The Retrospective and the **Prophet Soul** can work well together, but care must be taken by the Retrospective not to abuse the Prophet's willing and giving nature.

There will be the tendency by the Retrospective to abuse the good nature of the **Peacemaker Soul**, and to exhaust and drain their energy.

As long as the **Dreaming Soul**'s rose-colored glasses stay on and the Retrospective keeps their controlling nature in check, this relationship could work.

The Retrospective could underestimate, ignore, or undervalue the **Visionary Soul**'s sensitive and grounded traits, with damaging results.

There will be definite power struggles with the **Hunter Soul**, both signs showing demanding behavior and insensitivity, and though there will be times when it works well, there will be times of utter disaster.

The Retrospective might take advantage of the compromising nature of the **Seeker Soul**, and will have tendencies to abuse and misuse, underestimating the Seeker's strong nature.

The Hunter Soul

The **Seeker Soul** inspires the Hunter, and is able to be a good influence and enable them to act.

A match with a **Peacemaker Soul** works really well, although the Hunter might tend to override, to bully a little, to take advantage of the Peacemaker's passive and compromising nature.

The Hunter can underestimate the **Visionary Soul**, be too controlling, and not pay enough attention to their partner's emotional needs.

The Hunter can definitely become irritated with the **Dreaming Soul**'s unrealistic nature, and with their nonaction, becoming frustrated and feeling restrained, held back.

If not careful, the Hunter could abuse the **Prophet Soul**'s passive nature and be insensitive and thoughtless to their partner.

The Hunter will almost definitely be insensitive to the **Retrospective Soul**, and will dislike their negativity, their dissatisfaction, and their "poor me" attitude.

The **Traveler Soul** works well if both partners' goals are the same, but the Hunter could also feel irritation at the nonaction of the Traveler.

The Traveler Soul

An ideal partner for the Traveler is the **Retrospective Soul**, whose negativity inspires a desire in them to take actions for a better and more fulfilled life, encouraging them to be more positive, more fulfilled.

A good match is the **Dreaming Soul**, but too much dreaming can lead both partners to do things that are beyond their abilities, which would cause frustration and disappointment.

The Traveler will always be in danger of ignoring the **Visionary Soul**'s feelings, and will struggle with communicating affection and love, a real requirement of a fulfilled partnership for the Visionary.

Partnering with a **Prophet Soul** can be a passive exercise at times, and the Traveler may experience frustration through not enough diversity and therefore there will be a danger of becoming bored.

The Traveler could ignore the **Peacemaker Soul**'s emotional needs and abuse their compromising and giving nature.

For the Traveler there can be the feeling of being restrained by the **Hunter Soul**, and the inability to give the right amount of attention that the Hunter desperately needs, which will cause frustration that will cause clashes.

The Traveler and the **Seeker Soul** will tend to lead separate lives, flowing and floating, but this can work really well.

The Seeker Soul

The **Hunter Soul** is an ideal match, as both signs will respond positively to new and exciting ideas, and the Seeker will love the Hunter's can-do nature.

The Seeker will be inspired by the **Visionary Soul** but must take care not to ignore the Visionary's need for emotional interaction.

The Seeker will experience frustration, and confusion will occur, if the **Dreaming Soul** stays too much inside their own head or is overly unrealistic.

Impatience and lack of inspiration may occur for the Seeker because of the **Prophet Soul**'s passive nature.

There is a danger of the Seeker not seeing the emotional needs and family commitments the **Peacemaker Soul** so very much needs.

The Seeker will get along with the **Traveler Soul**, but if there are differing interests, both might live separate lives, which can be good or bad for both partners.

For the **Retrospective Soul** and the Seeker, there will be too much negativity, which both will find draining and oppressive, and flooding is possible.

It is easy to see from our examples of the Extrovert and Introvert energy signs, above, what causes those irritations and problems that can be harmful to our relationships. Each of us has our own abilities and inabilities to deal with another's traits. While some of us may find endearing qualities in a certain partner, others may find those same qualities will drive them up the wall. What makes one person crazy will make another person laugh hysterically. And what frustrates and angers some will inspire and create admiration in others. Why? Energy. It's as simple as that. Energies can flow the same way, blend, feed, and nourish, or energies can clash and drain and cause unhappiness.

Our Central and balanced soul signs are more able to blend, to flow. They have much less push and pull, much less need to demand, to force. So, what of those Central and balanced energy signs? Let's now look at them, and see what their likely responses would be to the other soul signs.

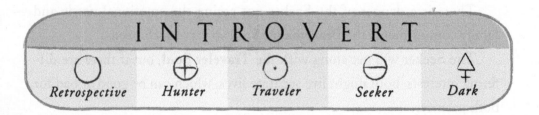

The Dreaming Soul

With the **Bright Star Soul**, there might sometimes be too much spark, too much fire, which would be draining and irritating for both, but the Dreaming Soul's rose-colored glasses can overcome those issues and allow for flexibility and acceptance.

For the **Dreaming Soul**, the Retrospective Soul can be a great match, unless circumstance forces them to take off their rose-colored glasses and see their partner's negative traits and controlling nature.

The **Warrior Soul** can be intimidating to the Dreaming Soul, and far too down-to-earth, causing the Dreaming Soul confusion and anxiety.

There could be some definite control issues with the **Visionary Soul**, and some standoffs.

The Dreaming Soul might find the **Hunter Soul** way too overpowering and controlling, also too realistic and down-to-earth.

A **Newborn Soul** could be an ideal mate for the Dreaming Soul, innovating, inspiring, but perhaps also a little unrealistic at times, and there is a danger that both could get too carried away and not be grounded enough.

The **Prophet Soul** could be calming and nonconfrontational and would allow for the Dreaming Soul's creativity and inspiration.

The **Traveler Soul** could be a good match, especially when both signs are dreaming the same dream.

The Dreaming Soul will find the **Old Soul** too grounded and can be flooded, overwhelmed, by the Old Soul's realistic outlook, which can put out the fire and dampen the Dreaming Soul's spirits.

There may not be not enough spark with the **Peacemaker Soul**; too little inspiration or motivation can dull the dream for the Dreaming Soul.

The Dreaming Soul may not give the **Seeker Soul** enough attention, and they will be confused as to why emotion is lacking in the relationship, and what it is they are doing wrong.

⊕

The Visionary Soul

For the Visionary, there could be frustration at not being able to satisfy the **Bright Star Soul**'s need for attention, and there are likely to be control issues, but these things can be worked out, and otherwise can be a good match.

Stubbornness from the **Dreaming Soul** could cause clashes and control issues, although otherwise a good match.

The Visionary could experience major control issues with the **Retrospective Soul**, and feel unfulfilled and hurt by the Retrospective's insensitive behavior.

The **Warrior Soul** works well with this sign, as both are able to inspire the other to take action, but clashes of will are inevitable, although they are usually resolvable.

For the Visionary the **Hunter Soul** could work well, but issues of sensitivity play a huge role, and clashing will occur if there is not enough emotional interaction.

The **Newborn Soul** can be fun, but there will be definite control issues due to the Visionary's frustration at the Newborn's undisciplined and unplanned behavior.

The Visionary tends to take advantage of the **Prophet Soul**'s good nature and to be insensitive toward their feelings.

The Visionary's sensitivity and need for emotional communication can cause issues with a partner who's a **Traveler Soul**.

With the **Old Soul**, inspiration, encouragement, and sensitivity go both ways, and the Old Soul is able and willing to feed the Visionary's needs.

The groundedness and family values of the **Peacemaker Soul** inspire and illuminate both partners.

The Visionary will feel a need to be emotionally fed, needing more interaction than the **Seeker Soul** can perhaps give.

The Prophet Soul

A great combination, the dangers for the Prophet are allowing the **Bright Star Soul** to use and misuse their good nature.

The **Dreaming Soul** can provide inspiration, although care should be taken to seek out action.

The Prophet is calming, feeding the **Retrospective Soul**'s need to be needed.

A relationship with the **Warrior Soul** can be exhausting, as the Prophet will find it hard to keep up with the Warrior's plots and plans, and all that action taking.

There is a need to watch control issues with the **Visionary Soul**, as the Prophet might be too passive and too pliable for their own good.

For the Prophet, allowing the **Hunter Soul**'s manipulative methods will cause major frustration, which may well result in aggressive reactions, which can be dangerous to both partners.

The **Newborn Soul** can work well with the Prophet, but it needs spark, work, and innovative action from both partners.

The Prophet will sometimes be too passive, which can cause nonaction and frustration for the **Traveler Soul**.

The Prophet may struggle with the **Old Soul**—too-high expectations and control issues.

A partnership between a Prophet and a **Peacemaker Soul** can be passive and low energy, which is good sometimes but not always and can cause frustration and boredom.

The **Seeker Soul** combination will take work from both partners to create an atmosphere of inspiration and active participation for the Prophet.

The Peacemaker Soul

The **Warrior Soul** is a great combination, as both are grounded and both are able to act through compromise.

For the Peacemaker, a relationship with a **Bright Star Soul** can work, but usually with great effort, as the Bright Star will easily use, if allowed, that compromising Peacemaker nature to the full.

The **Dreaming Soul** works well with the Peacemaker, but their ungrounded nature can cause frustration and impatience, and they will struggle with their inability to understand what makes the Dreaming Soul tick.

The Peacemaker may find a partnership with a **Retrospective Soul** exhausting, and frustrating for never being able to satisfy.

The **Visionary Soul** is a good match for the Peacemaker, as both are inspired by innovative ideas and creativity.

The **Hunter Soul** could work well, but might also be exhausted by too much compromising, if the Peacemaker allows it.

The **Newborn Soul** and the Peacemaker might inspire respect in each other.

The Peacemaker might find the **Prophet Soul** a little too easygoing, which could become boring.

The **Traveler Soul** is a good match, but care must be taken by the Peacemaker to not compromise to their own detriment.

Both the **Old Soul** and the Peacemaker inspire, both compromise, both reason, although there may not be enough action taken on either part.

The **Seeker Soul** inspires fun and excitement in the Peacemaker, but care must be taken to avoid too much compromising, which will cause the Peacemaker frustration and hurt feelings.

MIRROR IMAGE

As we have seen, there are many different soul-sign combinations; some work well together, and some do not. But there is one kind of romantic partnership that we have not yet considered. What if you were to fall in love with your almost-mirror image? A Bright Star with a Bright Star, a Prophet with a Prophet—how would those relationships work? Let's take a brief look and see the kinds of reactions each might have.

Retrospective–Retrospective

Two Retrospective Souls could work out if both were negative about the same things all the time; even then, though, it could be difficult. But if you are a person who really loves to be miserable, and there are people like that in the world, then here's a match for you. The Retrospective Soul is that kind of person, and would encourage those same tendencies in their partner. Of course, this pairing might result in a miserable old age, if the relationship survives that long, but if that's what those Retrospectives want, well . . . We've all heard the expression: Misery loves company!

Dreaming–Dreaming

Two Dreaming Souls could spell disaster in personal relationships, as there would be very little groundedness. However, if there were other good influences around them, people who were able to plan and strategize, to steer them on a solid and more grounded course, it could work. However, Fire signs don't take too well to being steered, or to abiding by other people's plans, so such expectations might be unrealistic.

Bright Star–Bright Star

Two Bright Star Souls could work extremely well if both are allowed, as individuals, to shine. For example, two movie stars, two politicians, or an actor and a doctor together could work well, each having a professional stage of their own where they could shine, where they could receive accolades and attention and be valued. The danger would be if one partner became more successful than the other, received more attention and praise. Then you would see a real explosion of emotions, and the struggle to maintain a good relationship would be great.

Hunter–Hunter

Two Hunter Souls can work well, both having great instincts, a great awareness of what they want from life, and a great understanding of what they need to do to turn their life plans into reality. Each is able to admire, energize, encourage, and motivate the other. If, however, their goals are different or if one becomes sick, or for some reason unable to play the Hunter Game—stalking and marking their territory, planning the hunt—then the other would move on without them, with very little feeling of guilt or remorse. Also, as with all Earth signs, even when both partners are feeling fulfilled, there will be those inevitable struggles at times for control.

Visionary–Visionary

Two Visionary Souls, like all the Earth signs, can really complement each other. They will admire and encourage their partner's creativity and sensitivities, and will also encourage each other to action, thereby motivating and at the same time being motivated, in very positive ways. But again, although to a lesser degree than the Warrior and the Hunter, there will be clashes of will, usually over control issues, and if the partners' goals and aims are not the same, this could cause those moments when one partner might feel the need to enforce a "change of plan" in the other. It would always be wise to tread carefully at those times.

Warrior–Warrior

Two Warrior Souls can work very well together, especially if their plans are the same, if their main goals coincide. They will have a lot of fun plotting together and will completely understand each other's needs and wants, and will work tirelessly together to achieve their aims. However, clashes of will inevitably occur, especially at those times when both partners want to be chief. For the Warrior, there always has to be one who leads and those who follow. As long as both partners realize this about themselves, and each other, and are prepared to give way from time to time, this can be a good combination.

Traveler–Traveler

Two Traveler Souls can work well together, especially if they earn or have enough money to do as they please. There would be no lack of excitement there, as they would always be willing to move or change, to try some new place or new idea. However, the Traveler's fickle nature and inability to settle down until they are older might be a problem, especially if one has reached that stage of maturity and the desire to settle down and the other has not. Then, watch out, as they will find that what they have often done to others—leaving, moving on, dropping, or disregarding their responsibilities—could happen to them.

Prophet–Prophet

Two Prophet Souls can really harmonize, really love the gentle and easygoing nature of their relationship. Each is able to honor and respect the other, to respect their passive and loving nature. With this combination you can expect few clashes, as both partners would generally strive to be there for each other. The only real danger would come if one decided they were bored and needed a little more excitement in their life, and the other had problems with this, liking the life they had too much to be bothered to change.

Newborn–Newborn

What a great time two Newborn Souls could have together. Fun, fun, and more fun . . . unless or until that dreaded word, *reality*, forced its way into the relationship. Both partners would be open and outgoing, each encouraging the other to play, but in the real world, unless they don't have to work, unless they don't have those worldly responsibilities the rest of us have—unless they have a real sense of owning up to responsibilities and taking necessary actions to fulfill those responsibilities, this combination of soul signs could be financially and creatively dangerous.

Seeker–Seeker

The combination of two Seeker Souls, as with all the Water signs, can work really well, especially if both are interested in the same things. Even if they are not, each is able to stimulate and to impress the other with their sense of curiosity, a need to learn, and the ability to know how to compromise in order to get their own way. Their knack of not getting too emotionally involved when they feel they don't need to, which is one thing that can ruin other relationship combinations, can really bring this potential partnership success. Neither partner needs to worry about a lack of sensitivity and neglect, as they don't take such things personally. So the pressures in this area are nonexistent, and both will understand, accept, and even be relieved that each one's emotions are under control.

Peacemaker–Peacemaker

Two Peacemaker Souls, like two Prophets, can really combine those wonderful Water-sign energies to make a great match. This partnership can absolutely work, especially if the people who surround them—family, friends, work colleagues—do not have too much influence on how each partner sees their role in their external environment. In other words, each partner must not allow the needs of family, friends, or work to override the needs of the other. This can happen, and then the one partner's needs are neglected as the other focuses on fulfilling the needs of others. Neglect and the inability to distinguish real needs, important issues, from more trivial and often attention-seeking ploys from outside the relationship can ruin even the best potential.

Old–Old

Two Old Souls are a great combination. Both are thoughtful of others, both balanced, and best of all, both need to compromise and see the other's point of view. The only real problems to worry about would come from that need to be fair, to be overly reasonable, to compromise in the extreme. A need for balance, for family harmony, is what both partners should strive for, and although it may take them a while to achieve their desired goals, Old Souls work well together and can do it.

NEVER AGAIN

So now we see how we might each react, how our energy compels us to react. We can see how, in the past, energy clashes affected our relationships that didn't work out. Misunderstandings, overreactions, anger, and frustration—all can be explained through soul signs. It's all about energy. But what about that energy? What is it that makes us go for the wrong type, the one, two, three, or more relationships we get into that are doomed from the start? Is it that magnetic pull, that unspoken, often unaccountable need to explore, to delve into dangerous territory?

Many souls desire excitement and challenge, and our opposites can be seen as exciting and challenging. Many of us are brought up in an environment of opposites, with a father, a mother, or siblings who act and react differently than we do. We learn to doubt ourselves, we learn that our differences make us less. We wish for acceptance. Why can't I be more like them? We have an unconscious desire to understand those feelings that make us different, and to figure out what it is that is wrong with us. Many of us have grown up with conflict, and so we find it hard to live without it, or to consider that perhaps we are worth more. Lacking self-worth, many of us don't believe that happiness is possible, or at least that it is not possible for us. So, subconsciously, we sabotage, we go for the exciting, the dangerous, the challenging, and we make choices based on what we have known, the examples we have been set, the lessons we have learned so well.

But it is not only those of us who come from abusive or traumatic childhoods who suffer bad relationships and bad choices. I have one friend I can genuinely say came from a wonderful home, with loving and caring parents and a close and loving sibling. Yet she too made bad choices in her marriage, and was tied to a tyrant of a husband for many, many years before she found the courage to divorce him.

"What attracted you to him in the first place?" I asked her.

"His power," she answered.

"But you knew his reputation and experienced his behavior before you married him," I said. "Why did you go through with it?"

"He reminded me of my father, who was loving and gentle and kind, but he had a terrible temper and would sometimes rant and rage, and really scare us all. But I always knew he loved us, and would do anything for us."

Many of us stay in bad relationships because of finances, or because we have children, or so we tell ourselves. We stay because we came from a great family and want to reproduce the experience, or we stay because we came from an abusive or destructive family and want desperately to produce something different, something better.

What possessed Hilary Clinton to stay with her philandering husband?

It certainly wasn't money. Was it power? A need to have a voice? A need for acceptance?

And what possessed Lucille Ball, our wonderfully funny and kind First Lady of Comedy, to stay with a husband who flaunted his mistresses and ignored and abused her?

What is it that makes successful people who have power in their own right stay in relationships that make them unhappy? The politicians, the businessmen and -women, those independently successful and wealthy people who can walk away from abusive relationships without thinking twice about how they will survive financially and in their careers?

How many times have we thought, "What is someone like her doing with someone like him?" or, "Why does he put up with that?"

What is it that makes us sabotage our own happiness and the happiness of those around us? The answer is really quite simple.

Learned behavior. That energy we have absorbed and retained from our past experiences. It plays such a big part in our lives, affecting the way we think, the way we feel, and the way we use or misuse our power, our energy force.

Damage was done to us in childhood, or through our first love, our first serious commitment, our first school, first job, our failures and successes. We all have damage. One friend I know was almost irreparably damaged by a teacher when he was seven years old; another, totally scarred by her father's sexual and physical abuse; one, by a loving and caring but controlling mother; another by his parents' seeming indifference to him as he was growing up. I could give a thousand examples, and still have thousands more. Some of these examples are totally traumatic, some seem insignificant by comparison, but to the one who is hurt, even the smallest of hurts can affect their self-esteem and cause damage. Even the smallest hurt, if we allow it, can grow into a monster that consumes us.

In my life I have had five serious relationships, five serious failures. Each time I wanted it to work, and each time I worked hard at making it last. But each time they failed, I failed, or so it seemed. By no means perfect, and doing many things wrong, I was certainly no expert in love. So who am I to know? Who am I to talk about how we find the right partner, the perfect match? And so I don't. Not me, not I, for I am not the one who knows, or at least not until now.

So I had five chances at happiness, and although not one of them worked, each taught me something valuable about myself. Aside from the first, when I was just seventeen, all were opposites, opposing forces, opposing energies: clash, clash, clash. What was it that made me head toward these disasters as opposed to running from them? In all truth, with my eyes wide open, and able to see clearly for the first time, it was me. It was me who, subconsciously, sabotaged my chances.

I look at myself, I look at all the people I know, I look at all the broken promises, the broken lives, the failed relationships that exist in a society which gives us so many resources and so many opportunities for growth, and these questions come to mind.

Why does anyone, in their right mind, stay in a relationship with someone once they find out that person is married and wants to stay married?

Why does anyone, in their right mind, stay in a relationship where there is physical abuse?

Why does anyone, in their right mind, stay in a relationship where there is emotional abuse and cruel behavior?

Why does anyone, in their right mind, suffer the tortures and indignities, the belittling or abusive behavior, or the lack of respect, the lack of valuing, from their partner?

Why does anyone, in their right mind . . .

And this, our "right mind," is the key.

Everything is energy. Our mind is energy: it absorbs energy, processes it, and becomes influenced by it. It holds on to it for future reference. Let me give you some examples, some personal examples of what I mean.

The girl is seven years old and for reasons she is never told, she is placed in an orphanage for a while. It's her birthday, but she doesn't know it until she is made to stand, at breakfast, while all the other children sing "Happy Birthday" to her. Then she is asked to go to the main table, where one of the grown-ups hands her a parcel wrapped in brightly colored paper. She feels confused, not in her right, or ordinary, mind. She doesn't understand the concept of birthday gifts, and is overwhelmed by emotions she is as yet too young to understand. This is the first of two times she will receive a birthday gift, until she is seventeen.

In that small experience, which lasts all of perhaps fifteen minutes, the energy of her emotions becomes processed, absorbed, and retained. Later, years later, she will analyze the experience and conclude that to her parents she is worth little.

The girl is maybe three or four years old, and standing in front of her father, small and afraid.

"Hold out your hands and let me smell your fingers," he says gruffly, and timidly she holds out her hands to him. It is morning, and she has been woken by her mother and hauled out of bed. This had become a usual pattern, and the girl knows what to expect. If, in her sleep, she had tucked her hands between her legs, then he would know, and she would be punished. "Go upstairs, take your pants off, lean over the bed and wait for me to come up." This was the standard punishment for any bad behavior until she was sixteen. Sometimes he would come up quite quickly, sometimes he might leave her there for an hour or two. Part of the punishment was in the waiting. Then he would beat her bare bottom, her legs, and her back, until she screamed.

Where was her mind? Was she out of it, somewhere else, somewhere safe? Not at all. Her mind, absorbing, processing, analyzing, and retaining, once again concluded she was of little worth.

Now sixteen, beaten almost to a pulp, her father enraged beyond the point of any self-control, her mother standing in the doorway, silent, watching, never lifting a finger to stop it . . . the girl's mind, absorbing, processing, analyzing, and now confirming what she already knows . . . her worth is nothing, she is valueless, and somehow very, very dirty.

Years pass, she grows, she needs to love and to be loved . . . at almost any cost. And so her choices are influenced by her inner and subconscious craving for acceptance and some small modicum of self-worth.

Through the years she learns, she realizes all these things; she knows where she has made her mistakes, and tries hard not to make them again. But so strong is the mind, the energy that the mind absorbs and retains, so damaging have her past experiences been, that her fear of rejection, now buried so deep within her as to have become almost unnoticeable, almost nonexistent, still influences her choices, and unknowingly, unwittingly, and so far unable to understand the energy which drives her, she subconsciously sabotages her chances. Just like so many, many, many of us do.

The alcoholic sabotages his chances of happiness. He does not, subconsciously, believe he is worth better.

The abuser sabotages his chances of happiness. He does not, subconsciously, believe he is worth better.

The victim sabotages his chances of happiness. He does not, subconsciously, believe he is worth better.

In the book *The Long Goodbye*, there is a line which reads, "There is no trap so deadly as the trap you set for yourself." How true that is, and this, subconsciously, is exactly what we do. We set ourselves a trap.

Opposites attract. That energy we subconsciously know will destroy us calls out to us. It is familiar, we have met it before, we know it, and it knows us. We know it won't work, subconsciously we know it won't work, but we are trapped by learned behavior, by what we know, and in its familiarity there lies a strange comfort, and also perhaps a challenge. Maybe this time we can beat it, or if not, at least understand or accept it. Or maybe this time it won't reject us, and we will become valuable at last. But it doesn't happen, our wishes don't come true, and happiness becomes an impossible dream. We have trapped ourselves with our need to find acceptance.

But acceptance *is* possible. Happiness, fulfillment, and a chance to value and to be valued is there for all of us, if we really want it to happen, if we can learn to understand our energy, the energy of our soul, that energy which influences our spirit, our mind, our being. Our driving force.

It's always the same. The past rises up to haunt you, often when you are least prepared to deal with it, when you are at your most vulnerable. The opportunity to learn and to grow presents itself again. Your soul calls out and speaks to you. Will you listen, or will you once again ignore the gift of pain?

She was in the shower, her hurt and tears unnoticed as water rained down. Small sobs escaped every now and then as she thought of yesterday. Not one question had he asked, not one. How was her day? Did she get the plants in the garden? What shall we do for dinner?

He had come home, talked briefly about his day, gone through to the living room, put on the TV set, and lay down on the sofa. As usual.

She had gone out for a couple of hours to have tea with a friend, and when she returned he was still in his place in front of the TV. As usual. Not one curious question, not an eyebrow raised in interest at where she had been, what she was doing, or how her day was.

In the kitchen she prepared a special dinner, perhaps in an effort to pique his interest. He didn't notice she was there, didn't ask what she was doing, oblivious to everything but himself. As usual.

A thousand, thousand times she had asked him, begged him, for some attention. He couldn't do it, it was not in his consciousness. He was not being mean or unkind, just simply and selfishly indifferent. As usual.

If it wasn't about him, then it simply wasn't happening. Go for a walk? What for? Spend the day in the garden? Why? Go to the movies? Only if it's something that he wants to see.

Nothing was any different than it had been for the last four years. So why was she hurt and crying? She knew perfectly well that if it wasn't about golf, or skiing, or him, then it wasn't of interest, it didn't exist.

Examples, too many examples, flooded her mind as the tears washed unnoticed down her face. And suddenly she was fifteen again, and in her parents' living room. She worked on Saturday mornings and had come home to an empty house, made a cup of tea, and was sitting quietly by herself when they rushed in the back door, laughing, giggling, shopping bags rustling. Into the kitchen they went, mother and three sisters, all talking, it seemed, at the same time. "Look at this!" and "See what I got," "Go try it on," "In a minute, in a minute, let's see the shoes first."

More rustling of bags, more chatter, but the girl sat very still, knowing she wouldn't be welcome in the kitchen. She wouldn't be welcome at all.

She sat, an outsider, staring out the window, trying not to feel, and saw her father go by. He glanced at her through the glass as he passed, then she heard the back door open, and her sisters, almost in unison, "Look, Daddy, see what we've got." The atmosphere in the kitchen was lively and happy . . . until their father spoke.

At a glance he had taken in the scene, knew instantly what was going on. "Where's Rosie?" he asked their mother, and immediately everything changed.

"I don't know," spat out the mother. "In the living room probably. I don't know."

"So you bought new things for everyone, did you?" It was more a statement than a question, and the girl, holding her breath, sitting very still by herself in the living room, could feel the anger and resentment rising in her mother and siblings, at her father's words.

"So then, what did you get for Rosie?"

The question was loaded, and hung silent and deadly in the air. They all knew that Rosie did not get anything.

The girl sat on in the living room, hearing every word, her hurt and tears unnoticed by everyone, as the drama played on.

"Nothing, nothing," spat out the mother, but with more venom this time, feeling caught out and furious at her husband's interference.

Time moved forward again.

In the shower, the old memory played over and over in her mind. No longer a woman of fifty, but fifteen years old again and hurting badly. And still, some things not changing, the hurt and the tears going unnoticed, as she had been. Unnoticed, passed over. Her mother had done it, time and again, deliberately hurting, deliberately mean. He had done it, time and again, not meaning to hurt, but indifferent just the same. And the result, for her . . . as usual.

When she had eventually begun to cook dinner, he'd finally made the effort to lift himself from the sofa. The bathroom was his first call, then the kitchen, where in an "I'm sorry for myself" voice, he said, "I'm not feeling so good; don't cook dinner for me, I'm not hungry."

If this were not usual, if the typical weekend scenario weren't two days of self-indulgence/golf/skiing/playing/drinking, if she were not used to seeing her living room used as a bedroom, if he did not usually sleep his afternoons and evenings away, and for all that, if he had only shown her the merest flicker of interest, asked at least one question, tried, if only feebly, to show her any attention at all . . . But she was drained of all feeling, except an incredibly deep ache somewhere in her chest.

She had taken her tray, a small dinner, to the bedroom, as usual, and spent the evening alone watching television, trying not to think. Each time she'd gone to the kitchen for a drink, she passed his body, prone, TV on loud, asleep or oblivious to anything but his own needs . . . as usual. She might as well have been invisible. He didn't see her at all.

Drying herself with the big white terrycloth towel she loved gave no comfort at all. Still she felt fifteen, with the past, come back with a vengeance, to haunt her. What was it that she must do?

Only one answer comes back, only one . . . Move on, move on, move on. No more time spent on self-pity. No more time spent on trying to figure out why. It was time to make a change. But she knew that change must come from within, or the same scenario would be repeated again in timeless motion as it had over the last thirty years. If she had known then about soul signs, it would have been different. She would have understood better, and understanding would have made it so much easier for her. Understanding that there is a driving force within us that compels us to act in certain ways, to be who we are, knowing that changes the way we think. Change the way you think and inevitably you change the way you act. Trying to change others to your way of thinking is a waste of time. And time, time, time, is a most precious commodity that few of us have enough of.

I don't believe in coincidence, and I don't believe in accidental meetings or unplanned circumstances, so I have to accept that every relationship, no matter how awful it might be, is an opportunity for the soul to grow. My relationship with an alcoholic and definitely a Retrospective Soul was no accident. Grey Eagle had told me of him through a dream vision at least a couple of years before I met him. As an Earth sign, I was attracted by his

Fire-sign passion. He was exciting. In turn, he was attracted by my ground-edness and my independent spirit. But he was an extreme Introvert energy, the opposite of my own Extrovert energy. Also, we each came from obviously strong and powerful energy groups—clash, clash. We were certainly meant to be, but does that mean he was my soul mate?

And then there was Andrew. With Andrew it was love at first sight. We both felt that we had met before, and, in a way, we had.

"Cross my palm with silver, dearie, and I'll tell you your future," the elderly woman had said. She quite surprised me with her request.

I was thirty years old, my daughter was six, I was still married . . . and would be for the next four years. I was working at the time, part time, as a shop fitter, and was stripping out one of the windows of the store I was working at when she came in. The manager of the store and her assistant were over by the far wall and I was by the window, closest to the door—an easy target.

I shook my head ruefully. "I'm sorry," I said, trying to be polite, "but I don't have any money." A good excuse, and also very true.

"Oh, come on, dear, just a small coin will do. I've been on my feet all day and could do with a rest."

She wasn't at all my idea of a gypsy, a fortune-teller, wearing a simple green raincoat, looking quite ordinary.

"Really, I'm sorry," I replied kindly. "I really don't have any money, but I can make you a cup of tea, if you'd like."

I made the tea, which she drank, and after a few minutes' chat, smiling, she said, "Well, come on then, let me tell your fortune anyway."

This was my first time, and I don't mind telling you, I was nervous. I was skeptical, and I was afraid to say no.

We sat opposite each other in one of the small dressing rooms, and I kept my head well down so that she wasn't able to read my face.

"What's wrong with your left side?" she asked. Without waiting for a reply, she added, "You've got problems with your left side."

My head shot up, I couldn't help it. How could she know? Two major surgeries, and the removal of my left kidney.

"You're married"—it was a statement, not a question—"and you have one child, a girl." A pause . . . and then, "And your husband has a red car."

Maybe she knew me, but I knew she didn't.

"You are going to meet a man, a man with a white car. He will be important to you, and you will love him, but he will be no good for you, no good at all."

I felt my stomach lurch. I was married, wanted to stay married, but she did not hesitate, was so sure.

"He will be a traveling man, a tall man with dark hair, and you will both fall in love."

It was four years later when I met him, and the moment I looked into his eyes, I knew him.

He was tall with dark hair, and his work, I discovered later, took him all over the country. When I met him again, he drove up in a white car, and at that moment, someplace in the recesses of my mind, I remembered the gypsy's words—and her warning. But it was already fated, meant to be. It felt right. The truth is, I had fallen for him the moment I'd seen him.

We knew each other. It was a match. And now I understand why I knew him so well. We were both Earth signs. Our energies connected us like magnets. We recognized ourselves in each other. Of course we did—we were created from the same source, the same power. However, our relationship would have taken real maturity and hard work, as he was my opposite—there was great attraction, but also great opposition. Andrew was a Hunter soul, an Introvert soul sign; I was an Extrovert soul sign: the same energy force pulling in opposite directions. Now, because we were from the same source, the same pocket, does this mean that Andrew was my soul mate? Might he have been my helpmate? Was our connection one of those inevitables, designed to help us both in our soul's growth process? Or was Andrew simply my playmate?

Yes, it was a match, two souls from the same pocket of energy instinctively knowing this. And as there are no accidents, no coincidences, I believe that Andrew was my playmate, my helpmate, *and* my soul mate. He came into my life, and I into his, to feed our souls at a time when our souls were desperately in need of nourishment. The experience helped me to become more mature and more understanding of circumstances that perhaps before I would have been far too judgmental about.

There is no doubt about it. Finding the right soul group and soul sign for someone else can be far easier than finding it for yourself. I think it's because we can be far more honest, we look with clearer eyes, and can be less judgmental.

The house I grew up in was full of Fire and Earth signs. The elemental forces of Fire and Earth were prevalent, and in fact, of the six children and two adults in the family, there was only one other elemental force present, which was the energy force of Air. There were no Water signs, no compromisers in this family. The combination of these soul signs certainly made life hard for all of us, and there was always an emotional scene of some kind being played out, as my mother, often most definitely the instigator, a Fire sign, was continually needing attention and drama. Now, not all Fire signs are like this, by any means. My mother's behavior was extreme, even for an extreme energy force, and she was volatile and unstable at the best of times, and her upbringing and learned behavior were part of the many reasons for that. But because she was a Fire sign, driven by her emotions, she had great difficulty controlling those emotional highs and lows.

Terry, the oldest of the children, was also a Fire sign, and could also be extremely volatile, especially around my mother and other brother, Malcolm, an Earth sign, a Warrior, like myself. Battles of one sort or another were always raging between them, and my father, an Earth sign, always trying to be in control, often found himself caught in the middle.

My father had a big fat bottom lip, which had a line going down the middle, almost dividing it in two. As a child, I was fascinated with my father's face, which always looked beaten up, and I would sometimes stare at his lip and wonder if mine would grow the same way. Years later, I discovered that my father's split lip was the direct result of my brother Terry throwing a metal dustpan, from a distance, into his face—one of the many dramas my mother was responsible for.

Five feet one inch and a little bit, very skinny, with no meat on her bones at all, my mother once took an axe from a nail in the garden shed and tried to break down the door to my brother's room, where, at age sixteen, he had barricaded himself, afraid of what my mother might do to him. Who knows what small incident had led to her rage. He was a teenager, with teenage be-havior, a know-it-all, and had dared to argue.

Every Sunday morning he would start a fight with his younger brother. Two years apart, born on the same day, one a Fire sign, one an Earth sign. My mother had taught them to hate each other, and, liking the drama, she had taught them well, even encouraged their animosities.

Terry was in prison a couple of times, both times for the same reasons: fighting, brawling, and drunkenness. He was the only man I know who came down the aisle for his wedding with his bride waiting for *him* at the altar, and he cried, loud sobbing sounds, every step of the way. A story too long to tell here.

In his twenties he met and was influenced by a good friend to channel his emotional energy in more positive ways. He became passionate about classical music, the opera, and the ballet. He paid for me to take singing lessons and piano lessons, and for a time I became the focus of his attention. Of course, it helped that his girlfriend at that time was a piano teacher and he wanted to impress her as much as he could.

For a time he lived at the YMCA, and I would visit him there on Saturday mornings. He took me to see my first ballet, *Coppelia*, and like him, I was entranced.

Finally, as I said, he married and settled down, had four children, and was a good father and husband, until his wife ran off with the deliveryman and took the children with her.

Totally heartbroken, feeling passionately betrayed, having tried to get custody of his children and failed, my brother went to work in the tin mines in Rhodesia, now known as Zimbabwe.

Driven by his emotional energy force, not having been taught any skills with which to reason, and unable to compromise, driven entirely by his emotions, he deserted his old life, his family, his children, and headed down a black hole. It was a journey that was to last him the rest of his life.

He was nearing his seventies when he finally came home to England, with no money, no property, and only the clothes on his back. And AIDS. He had AIDS. And he also had cancer.

He died a few months ago. It will be his birthday in a couple of days, which is probably what set me to thinking about him. He is a Fire sign, given from birth bad direction, and bad example. He had lived in confusion for most of his life. But he was my brother, and he had a heart as big as a house. Full of love, and with no idea how to express it, life for him always seemed to come out wrong. He truly loved his children, and I hope one day they will know it. I hope one day someone will tell them about his generosity, and above all, his kindness and his passion for life.

Family life can be difficult for everyone, as the mix of energy, the driving force of each family member, can create disharmony.

My brother felt guilt and remorse for most of his life, first because of his relationship with his mother. He should have tried harder. Done better. Acted differently. His lack of self-esteem, his guilt at the way he treated her, his confusion and hurt at the way she treated him, these things played on his mind and made him miserable. He never did get to understand any of it. He never did get to forgive her, or to forgive himself. Maybe now, though, maybe now he can.

My brother was a Bright Star Soul, a Fire sign and an Extrovert energy. He needed attention just as much as a man in the desert, dying of thirst, needs water. From the beginning, even as a small boy, he needed to be noticed, and if he couldn't get that attention one way, then he would get it another. This was his Fire-sign energy force. He wasn't bad, tried so hard to be good. But due to his upbringing, his environment, and the combination of soul signs in our family, the inevitable happened. He simply couldn't help it.

Our mother was a Retrospective Soul, an Introvert energy, and also a Fire sign. Their relationship was inevitable: clash, clash, clash. Two powerful forces, emotionally driven, one having power and control over the other for many years; the other, inevitably rebelling against this.

Our father was a Warrior Soul, an Extrovert energy, just like him, and because of this they seemed alike in many ways. Their clashes came as my brother got older and wanted to be more in control of his own life. Both of them wanted to be the boss. In this, they clashed, especially because they were in close proximity to each other. As soon as my brother left home, his relationship with our father improved dramatically. Not so the relationship with his mother. That relationship was never fully resolved.

I have heard so many people talk about their difficult relationships with their parents. I have seen so many people holding on to pain, to disappointments, and to old hurts.

The reality is that whether or not we have good relationships or bad, when it comes to our parents, our siblings, or ourselves, there is much of our behavior that is easily explained. It is not about who favored whom the most. It is not about what is wrong with those of us who seemed not to be loved, who seemed not to be liked. The truth is, the way we behave, the way we act, has little to do with personal preference and everything to do with energy.

There are certain energies we respond to well, and there are certain energies we respond to badly. It's as simple as that. We are who we are, born into our different pockets of energy, having our own unique energy source. We are who we are, and we are acting in character. There are times when we just can't help it.

I love my brother, and I hope he sees this as a tribute to him and to his life. A soul, so misunderstood by others, so misunderstood by he himself, for most of his life here on earth. Now I understand, and only love him more.

ALL CREATURES GREAT
AND SMALL

I would like to end this part of the book on a subject important to me, and also to many of you. Without it, something special would be missing from our lives.

The last chapter showed examples of my personal relationships. Now I would like to give a few examples of some very different relationships; different, but just as important, and relationships that really bring balance to my life.

We are a soul cluster, a human soul cluster, born to this earth to interact, to learn to communicate, to have our learning experiences with those souls who are connected to us by their same or similar characteristics, which unify us as a race. We know how our planet is influenced by the five pronounced and primary energy groups, and how each of us is affected by them, but there is so much more life on this planet than us human beings. What of the animal kingdom? Are the creatures of our planet affected by our elemental energy sources also? The answer is yes, of course they are. Every living thing, every animal, insect, bird, reptile, plant, microbe on the planet Earth, is created by the energy of Fire, Earth, Air, Water, or Sulphur.

Those of us who are animal lovers, and I count myself among that group, will be fascinated by the concept that our beloved pets have soul signs, just like us. This applies to every living creature, and although I must leave the subject of animals, and their soul connections to their human companions for another book, still I thought it might be fun to give you some examples, just to show you what I mean.

I am a dog person, and so although I love most animals, many of my personal examples will be those doggie tales we all love to hear about. But I will try to find examples of other pets too.

Soul groups and soul signs have nothing to do with the particular breed of cat, dog, bird, or horse, just as soul groups and soul signs have nothing to do with race, creed, or color. But with animals it is easy to fall into the trap of categorizing by breed. For example, it is easy to think of Labrador retrievers and King Charles spaniels as Air signs, because they are known to be passive, friendly, and easygoing. It would be easy to think of whippets, poodles, and terriers as Fire signs, because generally they are known to be high-strung and emotional. German shepherds, Saint Bernards, and Dobermans might easily be mistaken for Earth signs, and our mixed breeds might too easily be categorized as Water signs, seen by some as compromisers. And of course, any mean, aggressive, or vicious dog would slip very nicely into the category of a Sulphur sign. But that is not how it works. Each individual creature was created in a certain place, at a certain time, and was influenced by its own particular primary energy force. So when we are looking to determine our pet's soul group, breeding, training, and environment have nothing whatsoever to do with it.

Now, it so happens that my Labrador is, in fact, an Air sign. Not, however, because he's a Labrador, but because he is passive, except at those times when he feels that I'm in danger, and then he will definitely show the aggressive side of his nature. Mostly, though, he is extremely easygoing, although he can get just a little temperamental, a little jealous, if I give too much attention to Rosie, my Brittany spaniel. It is obvious to anyone who knows him that he is a mama's boy, as he follows me around and is always either at my feet or under them. It is also obvious that even though he weighs around seventy-five pounds and stands about thirty-some inches high, he really is just a lovely little boy. He loves to play, he likes to go for walks and to explore new territory, he is very inquisitive, and he delights in new people. Everyone loves him.

As there are only three soul signs in each energy group to choose from, Niño could be a Newborn Soul, a Prophet Soul, or a Traveler Soul. My little boy is definitely a Newborn Soul.

Rosie is a different kettle of fish altogether, an English expression I'm sure you'll appreciate, given the title of this chapter! Just watching her, I see how her mind is always working, even when she's having fun. To her, fun is trying to catch the frogs in the pond, or sniffing out mice in the snow, any outdoor activity where her strategizing mind and her incredible single-minded planning are working at their best. Definitely an Earth sign, absolutely taking control as much as she is able of her own life. Her choices, or rather mine, as I try to work out which soul sign she is, are the Warrior Soul, the Visionary Soul, and the Hunter Soul. I can eliminate the Visionary Soul, as the Visionary, remember, has a Central and balanced energy. Rosie has an extreme and obvious energy. Now it would be really easy for me to assume that she is a Hunter, especially as she has been bred as a hunting dog and is very good at it. This is where I have to be careful, and to pay closer attention to my puppy's character traits.

Yes, she does have many of the traits of the Hunter Soul; however, unlike the Hunter, she has extreme Extrovert energy, and although she loves the outdoors and adores the hunt, she is a very gentle and a very protective little character. She was once in the most outrageous and vicious dogfight, solely in defense of Niño.

Recently Rosie underwent a terrible ordeal, a tumor on her right foot, and had to have her front right leg and shoulder removed. Her speedy recovery amazed everyone, as she woke from the anesthetic and immediately stood up. Within two weeks she had mastered her balance and was swimming, frogging, planning, and strategizing. Still, she wanted her cuddles, needed attention, and did not want to be too far away from me. Very sensitive, and extremely protective and caring, Rosie is definitely a Warrior Soul.

Because I am really enjoying myself with this chapter, I would like to give just one more example of my own dogs, even though I could dedicate this whole chapter to them very easily.

Karma and Jasper were both King Charles spaniels, half brothers, and a lot alike in many ways. But one was very much an Air sign, and the other most definitely a Fire sign. Karma, the Air sign, was easy to please, and wanted desperately to please everyone. Unlike Niño, Karma was not really a dog who liked to play, or cuddle, or sit on a lap, although this breed of dog is renowned as a lapdog. Karma was simply a pleaser, a live-and-let-live kind of guy, and those of you who now know your soul signs should easily recognize which one he was. A Newborn, a Prophet, or a Traveler? No doubt about it, a Prophet he was, and of course, although he passed several years ago, he still is.

Jasper, on the other hand, was definitely a lapdog, a little temperamental, definitely driven by his emotions, with a distinct fiery streak, and although he was the younger dog, he tried almost from the beginning, as a puppy, to be top dog. A Fire sign, driven by his emotional needs, which one of our three choices was he? A Bright Star, a Dreaming Soul, or a Retrospective? We can easily eliminate the last, as he was a pleaser too, with Extrovert energy. We can also eliminate the Dreaming Soul, because Jasper, no matter what, made sure he was the center of attention, and would get up to all kinds of tricks to gain everybody's attention. And he usually did, playing the stage and being the star. He was a tough and savvy little Bright Star Soul.

Okay, now for some other animals I have known which were not my own. A Wheaten terrier whose temperament was so outrageous, temperamental to the point where his mistress had to resort to doggie Prozac, and I'm not kidding. Loving, adoring, and viciously (and I do mean viciously) protective of one person and one person only, his mistress, he was mistrusting and often aggressive to others, even to people he knew well. He was especially difficult around men, and his pet psychologist explained to my friend, the owner of this puppy, that her dog considered himself to be the man in her life, the master of his household, and the guardian of his treasure: her. Without question a Fire sign, his emotions driving every move, and certainly a Retrospective Soul, always expecting perfection and finding that perfection in one source only, his mistress.

A golden retriever, who at first glance may seem to be an Air sign, like Niño —friendly, happy, and craving affection. But when you get to know him better, he will very quickly show you that he is not really as easygoing as he seems. In fact, Farley—that's his name—really quite likes his own way, but has a way of getting what he wants by evaluating a situation, and by compromise. When commanded to sit, and to give up the slipper, he will easily and willingly obey the first command but ignore the second, tightening his grip, and will wag his tail to show that, well, the slipper is really his now, isn't it? "Let's play fair," he is saying. "Something for you, something for me." Watching the way he is, seeing how cleverly he manipulates each of the members of his family, using different techniques to win over each one, it becomes apparent that he is a Water sign. But which one? An Old Soul? No, I don't think so, and this time, because he is not my dog, and I don't see him that often, I am making my assessment partly by instinct: I don't think he's wise enough. Nor do I think he is a Seeker, as there is nothing reserved or introvert about his energy. It is because he really knows how to please each member of his family, and because it is apparent that he is trying his best to please them all, that I think perhaps he is a Peacemaker Soul. Maybe his owners will let me know if they think I'm right. I'm pretty sure they'll agree.

Now I am going to give a few examples of cats. Cats, of course, are known to be really independent, and there are quite a few soul signs which are not that way at all.

Growing up, we always had a cat, a black-and-white cat named Whiskers, who lived to a ripe old age. In thinking about which type of energy he would be, which soul sign he would be, there are two I would immediately have to eliminate. Whiskers was not a cat driven by emotion, not by any means, nor was my childhood pet a passive and easygoing creature, although you might have mistaken him for such as he lay curled up in his favorite spot, on a winter's evening, on the rug in front of the fire. So he was definitely not a Fire sign or an Air sign.

Whiskers was smart and cunning, as many cats are, but allowed himself to be stroked and petted by my sisters and me, even though sometimes his tail swished and twirled, and he made the occasional hissing sounds of disapproval from time to time. He was a compromiser, and as long as he could have what he wanted, his place on the rug, he would allow the petting to continue, although he would only tolerate so much before he batted you with his claws.

He was a Water sign, but which one? An Old Soul, a Peacemaker, or a Seeker? Definitely not a Seeker, as he did not really pay attention to anything very much; he was not at all a curious cat. Nor was he a Peacemaker, as he was really not too interested in the affections of the family, except for my older sister. An Old Soul then? It seems, as I remember him, that he was quite a wise and knowing animal, with many of the Old Soul's traits:

knowing what made him happy, and perfectly able to fulfill his own needs.

Then there were Tabatha and Thomasina, who found their way into our lives when Samantha Jane was five. "We have to save them, or they're going to be drowned," my child wailed, as she raced into the kitchen one day, repeating what my neighbor had just told her. My neighbor, of course, knew just what she was about. What could I do?'

They were sisters, but very different. One, a show-off, proud, if not a little arrogant, and really entertaining, definitely living high on her emotions. Thomasina would lash out, biting and scratching, very much a Fire sign. Too content to be a Retrospective Soul, too much of a show-off to be anything other than a Bright Star.

Her sister, Tabatha, was much more calm, much more independent, definitely a strategizing Earth sign, always out, looking for the next meal, the next tasty morsel she could hunt down, then moving on to greener and more fruitful pastures. There's no doubt about it, she was indeed a Hunter Soul.

Moving on, I'm going to attempt one more species, this time horses. For these examples, though, I will have to rely on the owner's knowledge, as horses, though they impress me greatly, are not a category of animal that I know anything about. So I am going to rely on my friend Esther Capen, most definitely a horse person, who has owned and been around these animals all her life.

It was a Tuesday morning, Esther's day off, and we were both at the site of the new healing center. I had thought initially that horses would be difficult for me to assess. I don't know why, perhaps I hadn't realized that horses have such a diversity of characteristics and personalities. You horse people out there have to forgive my ignorance; as you'll see, I know better now.

My session with Esther couldn't have gone better. I listened, enthralled, as she recounted story after story. Here are just four examples.

Whiskers—yes, the same name as my cat, long since gone—was a kind and gentle horse, nice to be around and with a good attitude. He was blind in one eye, something that might have fazed some horses, but Whiskers apparently was able to compensate easily: He was a great compromiser. "If you were riding him in thick ground, he would always look for the best way to go." If John, Esther's husband, wanted to ride him one way, and Whiskers felt differently, he would let John know, and "if you gave him his head, you would see that the horse knew best, and he would do his best." As I was listening to Esther, I realized that Whiskers was definitely a Water sign, an evaluator and a compromiser. But which one? Then Esther said, "He's sensitive, sensible, and very wise." An Old Soul, no doubt about it.

Pepper, horse number two, just had a foal. "She is inquisitive, calm, even under stress, is really sensible and very grounded. She observes everything," says Esther. "She is a planner and she definitely strategizes. In fact, you can literally see her thinking." Sounds like an Earth sign to me, and of course, we have a choice of three. "The other day three deer came into the pasture, and Pepper was hitched. She turned her head to look, and did not run to them, but walked slowly and carefully, strategizing as she went."

One day Esther lost a horse; it went missing from the pasture. Pepper was neighing loudly, and Esther asked her to help find the lost horse. She held Pepper's reins, and Pepper guided Esther to a nearby creek. There Pepper stopped, laid her head over Esther's shoulder, pointing in the direction of the stray, and whinnied loudly to the lost horse, who heard, and came.

I asked Esther what she felt Pepper's strongest traits were, and gave the descriptions of the three Earth signs. "Oh, a Warrior, most definitely," she said. "Pepper is extremely protective of her foal, and of the other horses we have. She's a leader. Most definitely a Warrior soul."

John Morgan was easy. "A horse definitely driven by his emotions, he has spells, and just takes off when he feels like it. You can't trust him, as he must always have his own way. Life is about him, his needs, and he lets his emotions control him. Very skittish—a shadow, a butterfly, a bird, anything can set him off. It may not be anything, just something in his head. He's very emotional." No guesses for this one. John Morgan is obviously a Fire sign. "Not a Retrospective," says Esther. "He's too happy and contented. Could be a Dreaming Soul, but wait . . . He likes to be number one, and gets jealous if the other horses get attention over him. He always comes to you, no matter what, needs attention all the time, and loves to be the center of activity. A Bright Star. I'm sure he is."

"Comanche . . ." And as she says his name, Esther's voice softens just a touch. "He has soft eyes, is a thinker, and wants to please. Very easygoing, easy to train, extremely loyal, likes to be out but he is happy to be anywhere. Sounds like an Air sign to me," Esther comments, now really getting into the soul sign thing.

"Okay," I say. "Which one?"

"Well, he has a really nice attitude, is unobtrusive, very calm, placid, committed to his trainer and his training, very quickly gets his head down to paying attention, does what is asked of him, and enjoys doing what he's asked."

I again explained the character traits of the three Air signs.

"Definitely, most definitely the Prophet," Esther replied, no hesitation in her voice at all.

So, you can see, animals have soul signs too. Dogs, cats, and horses were my examples, but I know that many of you have different pets, other kinds of animals, and you are perhaps wondering if the same thing applies to them. Even the smallest molecule is a certain type of energy, born of, and created from, one of the five main energy sources: Fire, Earth, Air, Water, or Sulphur. So yes, you can apply soul signs to any creature, and in particular, to your own pets, as it is you who knows best what traits, what characteristics, they have, and what type of energy drives them.

The one example I have not given here is that of Sulphur, although there are, indeed, purely evil creatures who live among us on this earth plane, some of them, yes, even someone's pet. Now, that should put the cat amongst the pigeons! I just felt that here in this chapter it was not appropriate to discuss them. Maybe in the next book, Grey Eagle will tell us more about them.

For some of us, our animals are an important and integral part of our lives. That is how it is for me. For others, animals do not play nearly such an important role, and that's okay too. We are who and what we are. But no matter how you might feel, and no matter what preferences you may have, animal or human, we are all of us souls, all creatures living together on a planet which gives us life, experience, and understanding. All of us—all creatures great and small.

I AM!

We all, even animals, have our earthly experiences, and we retain the energy of those experiences. We absorb, we process, we become influenced by that energy, and our driving force is made more powerful—more powerfully destructive or more powerfully constructive. And this is our choice.

Which will you choose? Will you let your knowledge of soul signs help you, as it has me? Will you see that there are truly some things about yourself that you simply can't change, and that it's okay? Will you see that there are truly some things about your partner that he or she simply can't change, and that to try to change those things is only going to sabotage your chances of happiness?

Are you a wonderful Fire sign? A Bright Star, a Dreaming, or a Retrospective Soul?

Are you a grounded Earth sign? A Warrior, a Visionary, or a Hunter Soul?

Are you a gentle Air sign? A Newborn, a Prophet, or a Traveler Soul?

Are you a peace-loving Water sign? An Old, a Peacemaker, or a Seeker Soul?

No matter what soul sign you are, we are all deserving of happiness, and we are all deserving of being loved, and we are all deserving of being ourselves.

Happiness, love, self-worth. How can we find these things? Simple. Know yourself, follow the rules and keep to the guidelines. Hope and happiness are just some simple steps away. Never again do you need to doubt that all these things can be yours.

When we are emotionally crippled, we feel the need to fix or to revisit the past. We need to feel loved and accepted by the same type of people who, in our past hurt, rejected or abused us. We think, subconsciously, that by finding that acceptance we will somehow heal, that it will heal our soul, but it doesn't, it doesn't work. It never really works. Why? Energy. Remember, it's all about energy. Those same types of people, those same soul signs, are those whose energy is completely incompatible with ours. And we can never change that, no matter what we do or how hard we try.

Opposing energies may well attract. They may well be challenging, exciting, and fun—for a while, at least. But they will always and inevitably clash with our own souls. Always. Seeking ways to heal, to fix ourselves, our hurts, our pain, our lack of self-esteem by falling into the same relationships, going for those same soul signs, over and over again, will only damage us more and cause us to be even more confused. So we must let go of who we might wish we were, who we might wish our parents, our siblings, our partner, our children, to be. We must let go of the "if onlys" and learn to live in the now, the present. Learn from the past and from your past experiences that you, and they, can only be driven by that force of energy that created us, our life force. Embrace this knowledge, this fact of life, and of life eternal. Embrace your power.

The best thing this knowledge can give you is yourself.

Who are you? You are a living, breathing force of power, an indestructible source of energy. Embrace your soul. Know your soul sign. Look for those whose energy is compatible with your own. Stop sabotaging your chances. Learn tolerance and understanding with those whose energy is incompatible with yours, and then . . . move on. Once you dare to be more of who you are, the less you will hold on to those who hold you back.

By now you will know your soul group, and you will know what soul sign you are. You need to learn to say, with true conviction and pride, and from your heart, "I *am!*"

I *am* a Retrospective!

I *am* a Dreaming!

I *am* a Bright Star!

I *am* a Hunter!

I *am* a Visionary!

I *am* a Warrior!

I *am* a Traveler!

I *am* a Prophet!

I *am* a Newborn!

I *am* a Seeker!

I *am* a Peacemaker!

I *am* an Old!

For the first time in my life, I truly know who I am and, more importantly, why I am. I have finally found the answers to all those long-asked questions which have haunted me since childhood. Knowing the answers does not change things that happened in the past, but it has changed my attitude toward myself, and also my attitude toward the people in my life who I was forever wishing could be different. Now I see, and I see clearly. He was a Warrior, she a Retrospective; he was a Hunter, she a Bright Star; and so on. I am not less because of this. In fact, I have become more.

For the first time in my life I know who I am, and I so hope that you do too. I can say, with true conviction, with pride, and from my heart . . . I *am*.

I *am* a Warrior Soul!

So then . . . who are you?

PART ✦ FIVE

THE END AND THE BEGINNING

fire   *earth*   *air*   *water*   *sulphur*

THE FINAL CHAPTER

Life is full of endings, for all of us, we know. Throughout our journey of soul signs, even as we come to understand our uniqueness and indestructibility, still we are fragile human beings, and our endings, especially when we are young, can seem devastating and totally destructive to our lives, to our souls. We break up with a girlfriend or boyfriend, we lose a job, we are forced to move, there's an accident or a burglary or a fight with a sister, a mother, a husband, or a father. Our endings can come on an almost monthly if not daily basis, and we wonder, "What am I going to do now? How am I going to survive?"

There are other endings, of course, which we see as blessings, as beginnings—God finally gave us a break. We get out of debt, we get a great job, we meet a new beau, a baby arrives, we buy a new house, a relationship is restored, and we wonder, "How can I be so lucky? What did I do to deserve such good fortune?"

We all live this way, with the good and the bad, the ups and the downs, and none of us is exempt. We call it life, for better or for worse, and none of us escapes . . . not even when we die.

No matter what our endings and beginnings are, we all handle them differently, driven by our own individual and unique energy source: Fire, Earth, Air, Water, or Sulphur power. Our power.

There is not one of us, not one soul on earth, who does not have power. Collectively, as a soul cluster, we can use that power in a good way or in a bad way. It's the same for us as individuals. We choose. We don't get to choose which energy source we are from, but we do get to choose what we do with what we are given.

All of us are flowers, wonderful golden daffodils, in a garden rich with light and power and opportunity. Like old soldiers, we never die, we just fade away. We fade away from this earth, from this garden, only to be planted in another garden even more beautiful and rich. Endings and beginnings.

Working for the last twenty-five years as a spiritual medium and healer, I have seen many people die, and I have spoken with many more after they have left this earth. That is what I do. This is who I am. This is how I have come to know and to understand soul signs.

I have sat with many as they have cried for their losses, their endings, and I have sat with them as they have cried and laughed, laughed and cried, as those in the spirit world have shown themselves again, in their new beginnings. Faded from our vision, but living and breathing just the same, only now in another place. Ending the way of one life, beginning the way of another.

For most of us, the greatest and most difficult endings come when someone we love dies. The final chapter. The end of a person's life. And for many of us, especially those who have lost a child, it seems like it is the end, the final chapter for us too. Life—or what is left of life—seems not worth living anymore. But yet we go on, going through the motions, trying hard not to let our grief overtake us completely, feeling like robots, moving through a sea of human actions and reactions, waiting for the fog to clear. And we wonder, "How can life go on? What on earth is the point? Why did God give us such pain?"

And so life remains something of a mystery, and even though we get the point—learning, growth, and all that good stuff—still we don't get it, because life is just not fair.

There is a great song by the vocalist Chris Rhea that says so much, and more eloquently than I can about the mysteries of life, and the questions and confusions we all have, and no matter how many times I hear it, I feel a lump in my throat at the simplicity and truth of the words, and the sensitivity in the way he sings. It's about a little boy who is asking his grandfather about why terrible things happen, and it's about the grandfather who then begins to have questions of his own, and wonders what he should say to his grandson. The grandfather, confused and hurt by all the cruelties of life, finally says to no one in particular, or perhaps to God: "Tell me there's a heaven . . ."

When I talk to people who have lost a loved one, I tell them there's a heaven, because I know that it is true. I tell them that each ending is merely a new beginning, as it is for all of us in any circumstance in our life. I tell them that in this heaven there are angels present, and that the light of God is visible to all of us. And I know this to be true, because I have been there many times.

In the western world, all stories have a beginning, a middle, and an end. For most writers, it is a rule: There must be a beginning, a good beginning, to capture the reader's imagination; a strong middle, to hold their attention; and an ending, as powerful as it can be so that the reader wants to find your next book.

When I begin writing, I never start at the beginning. My chapters become like pieces of a jigsaw puzzle, that at sometime down the road, with the help of my editor, I will piece together to make a picture. But still, there has to be a beginning, a middle, and an end. That's the rule, and we all have to follow certain rules, especially if we want to make some sense of what we are doing.

Native American culture is a little different. The beginnings of their stories are the continuation of their previous chapters, for they know that true life has no endings at all. There are no final chapters, not in their stories, or in their lives. Wise beyond imagination, their stories have no beginnings, no middle, and no end. This is life as it truly is.

So, in this final chapter, I am going to go back to someplace at the beginning of this book where I refer to my spirit guide, Grey Eagle, and how he helps me in my work. I am going to tell a story or three which are very relevant to life, to who I am, to what I do as a spiritual medium, and to soul signs.

Every time I talk with someone in the spirit world, no matter who they were in their earthly life, they teach me something. They teach me to intuit that I am a soul, that I am more than a human being. Ever since Grey Eagle introduced me to soul signs, each day I am reminded that I'm a Warrior Soul, and my actions resonate with this knowledge. Each day I look at others through new eyes, and I understand them better. That waitress, that businessman, that salesperson—immediately I feel much more tuned in to the person, they become something more to me, and I wonder what soul sign they are. There's also the sense of connecting with something bigger than us, something more than what we see with our eyes—something we can believe in. There are times in all our lives when we feel lost, and soul signs give us that great sense of knowing that we are not alone, that we belong, that we are thinking, feeling, acting, and reacting like others.

As a natural-born spiritual medium and healer, and as a Warrior Soul, I have a need to express this gift that I have, and the best way to understand my gift, other than experiencing it firsthand, is through my storytelling.

God's Plan

It was winter in Vermont, and a snowstorm was in progress. I had been with Llewella all day, since early morning, in fact, when I had gone to the hospital, arranged her transfer home, and then stayed with her, arranging nursing care and talking with her friends.

I had known Llewella for more than a year, and over that period of time we had become very close. Her illness was terminal, and we both knew it, and we had worked on improving the quality of the time she had left, rather than the quantity. Extremely spiritual, she knew the Bible by heart, as she had read it more than once a day all her life. Llewella had a great faith in God, and believed that He had sent me to her. Having that same great belief myself, I believed that God had given me Llewella for my benefit rather than hers.

The day before had been a nightmare. Cheyenne, Llewella's friend, had called in a panic. Llewella had been vomiting badly, and was complaining of pain in her stomach. I knew immediately that it was serious, as I had never before heard Llewella complain about anything.

"Call the nursing service and get someone out to the house. I'll be there as soon as I can."

It took me an hour, and the visiting nurse was already there when I arrived. "She's dehydrated, " the nurse said, "and we have to get her to the hospital right away."

"No," said the voice from the bedroom, firm and strong and still in control, typical of a Warrior Soul. "No, I'm not going to any hospital. I'm going to stay right here."

"She's stubborn," said Cheyenne. "You won't make her do what she doesn't want to do. No way."

I knew she was right. One of the things I had come to love most about Llewella was her cantankerous streak. It was what had helped her survive, working the farm as she had done all her life, on her own since her parents had died more than thirty years before. I sighed, took a deep breath, and went into the bedroom, closing the door quietly behind me. Llewella and I had to have a heart-to-heart talk, and I knew it wasn't going to be fun.

"You have to go, you know," I said, gently taking Llewella's hands in my own. "You're dehydrated, which is why you feel so bad. You need treatment, and we can't do it here."

The stubborn old woman looked right at me, her jaw set hard, and for the next ten minutes we talked it through, she giving me all the reasons why she should not go, me giving all the reasons why she should. The bottom line was that Llewella was afraid. Not afraid of dying, as some might suppose; no, she had come to terms with that a long time ago. But she wanted to die at home, where she belonged, where her heart and soul were, among things that were familiar to her, where she felt safe. She was afraid that if she left her home, she would not come back.

So we compromised. Two Warrior Souls, each having learned to trust the other, each loving and caring for the other's well-being, each with mutual respect. Finally she said, "I'll go, but only if you promise to have me back here in twenty-four hours. I don't want to die in that damn hospital bed."

"Twenty-four hours," I promised, and prayed to God that I could keep that promise. Instinct told me that I could.

Now, as I made her comfortable in the bed on loan for the time she had left, and made sure it was close enough to the window for her to see out onto her beloved farmland and her horses, it broke my heart to see how weak she had become in just the last twenty-four hours. Still, she managed one of her incredibly bright smiles as I looked down at her and tucked the blankets under her chin.

"You kept your promise," she whispered softly, and I nodded. "But only just," I thought, "but only just."

As I squeezed her hand, I knew that this was Llewella's last day, and selfishly I thought, "What am I going to do without her? What am I going to do?"

It would be fair to say that this tough old farmer, with big muddy boots, her pants held up with string, a cap always perched on her gray/blonde head, the peak pulled down over her weather-beaten face, her gait, until just a few short days ago, strong and purposeful, even when she had to use a walker—it would be fair to say that Llewella was an inspiration to everyone who met her. She was more than an inspiration to me.

Leaving as late as I could, knowing I had a lecture scheduled that evening and that the drive home would take at least an hour, probably more with the weather as bad as it was, I finally said my last good-bye. I knew I would not see her again on this earth.

The drive home was indeed difficult, and made even more so by the fact that halfway home I developed a really bad headache. My friend Joan, who was visiting from England, helped a lot by keeping my mind on the positives of dying rather than on the negatives of losing a friend, but still, by the time we finally reached home, my headache had swollen to mammoth proportions.

"Oh, God," I groaned. "Please don't let this happen. How will I be able to work tonight? All those people have traveled so far . . ."

Somehow, with Joan's help, I got dressed and headed to the school where I was appearing. It was a charity event, to aid a local children's facility, and I had been glad to agree to do it. But now, having driven through the snowstorm and arrived with less than five minutes to go, I was working myself into a real panic. The auditorium was full, with more than five hundred people present, all of them anticipating the best. My headache raged on, and my eyes were misty and out of focus with the pain. An image of Llewella flashed into my mind. God's plan, that was the important thing to remember—not Rosemary's plan, not the audience's plan . . . only God's plan was important here.

As soon as I began the evening, I felt the warmth of my audience. More than a third of the crowd had traveled from all over the country to be here. Some had flown, some had driven for hours, despite the appalling weather conditions, and even the locals had given up their log fires and cozy armchairs to spend the evening with me.

As always, I felt my guide's presence, and even though the headache still raged, I began to calm, to trust. "Whatever will be, will be," as the old Doris Day song goes. Que sera, sera.

I saw my first communicator quite clearly, standing next to her parents, and as I walked halfway up the hall toward them, she described the brain hemorrhage, the suddenness of her passing, and the ease with which she had passed. She was so pretty, with dark curly hair, shoulder length, pale olive skin, dark brown eyes, and a smile which lit up the room.

"I am a nurse," she told me brightly, "a children's nurse, and I really love my job."

Holding on to her father's hand, gently squeezing her mother's, I relayed all I saw and heard, and they nodded, and laughed, and cried, as their daughter gave them evidence of her survival beyond death.

Then, a tap on my shoulder, coming from the row behind.

"What about me, can I have a turn now?" Looking back over my shoulder, I saw a man in his early twenties.

"Of course," I said, smiling, still holding the hands of the young woman's parents. "Of course, go ahead. But who is it you want to speak to?"

"My mom," he replied boldly, "but you'll have to turn around because she's right behind you." He pointed to his mother, who was looking at me wide-eyed and incredulous that she had been chosen.

"Your son tells me that he died in a motorbike accident, that he hit a brick wall and died instantly, is that right?" I asked. She gasped and shook as tears flowed down her face, and she nodded that she understood.

"Your son is here, standing right in front of you, trying to let you see that he didn't die," I said softly, and she once again nodded her understanding, but as yet was unable to speak.

A tug from behind, and now again the young woman who had died of a brain hemorrhage was speaking, and standing next to her was a little girl, about five years old. "She's one of my children," I heard the young woman say, "and she has only been here a few days."

The young woman's parents were extremely confused when I relayed this piece of information, and for a moment, so was I, but confusion quickly passed as the five-year-old, quite determined to have her say, squealed loudly, and pointed down to the front of the audience. "There they are, there they are!" Quick as a flash, she made a dash down the hall to where her brother and sisters sat.

"Follow her, follow her," I heard Grey Eagle say, "no time for thinking, just go with the flow."

The "flow" took me to a time and a place not so very far away. I could smell the burning before I saw the glow, and I could see them, the ones from the house, before I saw their bodies, burned and blackened by the fire. A family of eight, parents, grandparents, siblings, and two grandchildren, one, my determined little five-year-old, the other just a baby, a few months old, a little boy. Eight had died in the fire, and I stood and watched with them as their house turned to ash and rubble, until nothing was left.

A tug at my sleeve, and I was moving again, coming back to the now. Sitting in front of me were two sisters and their brother, he just seventeen years old, and they held each other and cried as I recounted what I had seen.

Standing around them was a crowd, their family, who had died only a few days before, and as I looked toward the group, one large lady stepped forward to speak.

"I was a bus driver," their mother proudly told me. "I drove the school bus, I drove it for years." As she spoke, she cradled a baby gently in her arms, and, pointing to one of the sisters, said, "Tell my daughter we are keeping him safe, and that one day she will see her son again."

As I repeated the older woman's words, the young woman in front of me clung more tightly to her sister, a great wail of anguish escaping her lips.

My audience, too, was weeping, anguished by what they were hearing, hardly able to grasp the pain that these three young people had experienced.

I looked once again at the crowd surrounding them, and one by one I spoke with several others in the family who had died in the fire, all of them wanting to give messages of hope and of love. My audience was patient, but I knew I couldn't spend too much more time in this one place. It didn't matter. I knew I would be meeting with them all again, a few months from now, when they came to visit me in my home. For now, I could only be brief. The five-year-old was impatient, wanting to move on, and before I knew it, she had dashed back up the aisle to the young woman I had first spoken to, the young woman who had died from a brain hemorrhage, and pointing at her, she squealed excitedly, "Tell them she's my nurse, and we laugh and play and have lots of fun."

As I worked my way up and down the hall, wondering where I was to go next, I slipped into a time and place removed from my audience, and for a moment I was with my friend Llewella. As her face came into view in front of my eyes, I knew she had not yet passed. A few more hours still to go.

Then I was pulled away again, pulled back to the now. "I'm her sister," I heard someone say, "and I was sick with meningitis. It was very quick—a fever, my head hurt so bad, and then it was over."

I had come to stand in front of a young woman who was clutching at her husband in disbelief, hardly able to believe the accuracy of the message I was giving her. She nodded her head, swallowed hard, and blurted, "I've been asking and asking for a sign, for her to show me that she's with me. Could she give me a sign that it is really her? Could you give me a sign, Rosemary, that it really is my sister?"

Before I even had time to ask, her sister replied, "Tell her the bird, I was the bird, tell her I am the bird, the bird that has been coming to the kitchen window every day for the last few days. This is my way of showing her that I didn't die. Say to her, I am the bird that flies to your house, and taps its beak on the window, to let you know that I am always here for you." And the young woman in front of me gasped and cried, her heart overflowing with joy, for she understood the message perfectly.

"Go with the flow, go with the flow," said Grey Eagle, and I followed his guiding hand, on and on, to the next message, and the next, and the next, not thinking, just working, making the connections and letting it happen.

I am listening, and relaying a message, my head tilted to one side, my eyes focusing on what is beyond my "normal" vision, and then focusing on the person I am giving the message to. I move my head just a fraction to the right, and what I see takes my breath away. Standing next to his wife, a big smile on his face, and excitement in his eyes, is my friend, Sheldon.

I can't believe that I see him, and my heart takes a leap, and the lump that comes into my throat is huge. But why? I knew his wife was coming, I gave her the ticket myself. I feel tears threatening to spill down my cheeks, and I bow my head, biting my bottom lip hard, trying to gain some control of my emotions. Slowly, head down, I walk up and down the aisle. With luck, my audience will not see my distress. They will think I am listening for more voices, searching for more communication. In truth, though, I am merely a small and fragile human being who is floundering in a sea of mixed emotions.

Sheldon had been my friend. *Is* my friend. He had taken care of me, of my property, my dogs, my home. He had gone into the hospital for a simple surgery and was expected to return home the same day. I had been in Europe when it happened. I had returned to America to find him in a coma that lasted two weeks. I had gone to the hospital every day, staying close by, trying to be of some help to Mary, his wife, and also to the rest of his family.

It had been only six weeks since he had been gone, and although I had not actually seen him, I had heard him quite clearly on several occasions, particularly when he was instructing me to get his wife's Christmas gift, a chocolate Labrador, like my own. So now here we were, and here he was, and as I became more in control of my emotions, I took another peek. He was still there.

"Tell Mary," he said, "just tell her I'm here. She's hoping for a message tonight. And, Rosemary," he added, tears in his eyes, "thank you for the puppy. I love you, you know." It was all I could do to get the message out, and Mary was thrilled.

Now, once again, moving on, the energy flowing free and fast, the evening almost at a close, I went walking with my audience. The hall was full, a packed audience, despite the weather; the spirit world, filling and spilling over into the room, was an unseen audience, unseen by all but me.

So many, too many to count, but I knew the one I was to speak with next. He smiled, and stepping forward, placed his hand gently on his wife's shoulder, a small tear slipping down his cheek as he did so. Turning his head, he reached behind him with his other hand and brought forward a young boy, about ten years old.

"My son," he said, motioning to the child. "My son and I, we passed together, but Bridget," and he lifted his hand from his wife's shoulder to stroke the young girl's hair, "my daughter, had to stay behind."

"What happened?" I asked, already moving into that time-travel space. "What happened? " I asked Grey Eagle.

I saw two children, a boy and girl, riding with their father in the car. I watched the car and its passengers as they drove along the not-too-busy road, and heard the sound of their voices, laughing and chattering, the children playing some kind of game. Happiness is a wonderful thing, and I saw the father smiling as he listened to his kids, occasionally joining in the fun. A normal family outing. "It could be anyone," I thought, "it could be me and my child . . ." But my thoughts were cut short as my senses shifted and I felt it coming before it ever appeared in my vision. The crunching was loud in my ears, the sound of two vehicles colliding and rolling over, and over, and over again.

The boy and his father were floating, it seemed, as I watched, hovering above the wreckage. The girl too was floating, but in a different way, and separate from them. Then bright, bright light, and I heard whispered wings, the air about me moved, my hair lifted briefly in the breeze that they made as they scooped up the man and boy. . . . How many I could not tell, but the angels had come, and there was no turning back for them.

The ambulance lights were bright, the sirens loud, two lay dead, and one critical. She lay, small and crumpled and bloody, and I watched as they placed her in the ambulance and drove her away. Then, *wham*, time moving forward, I saw her as she lay in a coma, no one knowing if she would live or die.

Now, back in the present, I reached out and took hold of her hands.

Her father and brother drew close, giving words of comfort and hope, giving inspiration to the child, now thirteen years old, who still had such a long way to go to combat the disabilities the accident had left her with. She smiled as I gave her the messages from her father and brother, and the smile was wide, lighting up her face.

"Do they know I made it?" she asked, and I nodded.

"They do indeed," I replied. "They do indeed."

The evening was over, and what a spectacular evening it had been. My headache had dissolved like magic the moment I had begun to work, and I hoped I had not let anyone down.

It was two in the morning when I finally climbed into bed, and thoughts of Llewella came spilling into my mind.

"You have done all that you can do," Grey Eagle reassured, as I lay my head on the pillow. "It will not be long now, just an hour or so, and before you wake up she will be home. Angels are with her, and she can see them now, so go to sleep, don't worry, she is safe."

And I closed my eyes, as tears ran down my face, and I asked, "What am I going to do now?"

"Trust, little one, trust, for we keep you safe too. Trust, little one, trust, and you'll see."

So I slept, while my friend passed, and in my dreams she called my name. And I hear her words now, as I write: "God's plan, God's plan, God's plan."

Ryan

Chris is a Water sign, an Old Soul, and her husband, Mike, is an Air sign and very definitely a Newborn Soul. They have a good marriage and two great kids, Ryan, and Mia, who, by the way, just made the dean's list at the University of Vermont and is very excited about it. As an Earth sign, Mia is a real planner and strategist. Her feet are on the ground and she has a great relationship with both parents.

Ryan . . . Well, here is Ryan's story.

He was sixteen at the time of the accident, and a passenger in the car of a friend. The friend, and another boy in another car, thought it might be cool to race, without lights, to the end of the road.

There was no drinking, no drugs, just a couple of teenage boys fooling around.

The girl passenger in the other car testified later that she screamed and yelled at the driver to stop. She was terrified, she said, and thought she would be killed.

Ryan also screamed at his friend and tried to stop the game, afraid that there would be an accident. His friend took no notice.

They hit a tree going more than sixty miles an hour, on a small country road in Manchester, Vermont. The car rolled over, ending upside down in a ditch. Ryan also ended upside down, hanging by his seat belt with fatal head injuries, his life at an end, and so too the lives of his parents and sister—at least, the lives they had known until then.

Neither Chris nor Mike had given much thought to the idea of a life after death. Not religious, rarely going to church, and certainly rarely, if ever, paying that much attention to the ever-present possibility of death, now, suddenly and unexpectedly, they were facing it head-on. Each one, each a different soul sign, found themselves driven by their individual energy force, coming to some degree of acceptance of their tragedy, struggling for their new beginnings.

Mia, the planner, the strategist, the grounded Earth sign and action taker, made her plans and became involved with any and every activity that involved Ryan's friends. Her energy force drove her to keep busy, to keep active, to keep motivated. She became older and wiser than her years. She became even more grounded and more sensitive, and even though her pain is great, she found her new beginning. Her life is continuing, and in a really positive way.

Mike, the passive and easygoing Air sign, used to floating, to letting life take him where it would, found himself in unaccustomed downdrafts, states of depression that seemed unbearable. His energy force drove him forward but he continually gasped for air, trying to float above the pain and searing heartache. He eventually found his airspace again, able to be more his old self, but he never was able to return to who he used to be. He became more able to rise above the problems and difficulties that at one time might have brought him down, and he was able to lift himself to a place where the pain and torment of losing his son was a more bearable thing . . . at least for most of the time. He found his new beginning, his new way of life. Not better, by no means better, just different.

Chris, the evaluator, the thinker, a Water sign used to compromising, found herself in a stormy and somewhat uncompromising sea, a sea of thoughts, and feelings, and emotions she had never encountered before. There was no reason, she reasoned. There was no possible compromise, no life, no future, no hope. She was driven to feelings of emotional drowning;

she tried to swim but didn't want to, tried to drown but couldn't do it. Life, somehow, had to go on. But how?

If only she could be more accepting, like her Air-sign husband. If only she could be more active, take more action, like her Earth-sign daughter. "If only I could be more like them! Why aren't they more like me?"

From the beginning, almost from the moment she heard her son was killed, and even though she had never before given thought to life after death, Chris began to talk to her son. "Give me a sign. Just give me a sign that you're okay."

Each day she flowed, as all Water signs do, moving hour by hour, thinking, evaluating, a whirlpool of emotions, forced by the power of her energy source to try to find a way to compromise, to work with what she had, all the while asking her son for a sign.

The pennies came very quickly—her son's first sign. Pennies from 1983, the year Ryan was born. Chris remembered the game of "flip the penny" that her son continually used to play.

But still the river of emotion was torrential, the pennies were not enough, and Chris knew she needed help. It was her therapist who sent her to me. Or, perhaps more accurately, it was Ryan himself who guided his mother to a medium he could use to communicate through.

I have become friends with Chris and Mike over the last four years, and have spoken with Ryan on many occasions, and the evidence he gives of his survival after death is overwhelming. But my favorite, and the one which cast all of Chris's doubts aside, was the cactus. It was a simple enough message, but one that Chris and her family did not understand at all. Ryan began talking to me, and as he spoke, I felt myself moving to a place I did not recognize. I saw mountains and wild horses everywhere I looked, and then Ryan showed me a cactus, a small ground cactus that he told me was very special.

I recounted what I'd seen and heard, and Chris was very confused. She knew nothing about any of it, and when she recounted the information to her family and friends later, they were just as baffled as she was . . . until the following week, when Ryan's best friend, Andrew, returned home from a trip to Montana, from a place of mountains and wild horses. He and another friend had stopped to rest in a freshly mowed field, and as they sat, Andrew noticed a small ground cactus growing all by itself. Not another cactus in sight. With Ryan very much on his mind, and for no particular reason that he knew, he dug up the cactus and took it home to his mother—Chris's best friend, who immediately told him about Ryan's strange message.

Later that day, when Chris came home from work, she found Andrew in the kitchen of her home, the cactus held like a precious jewel in his hands. "I think," he said, tears in his eyes, "I think, Chris, this cactus is for you."

On Top of the World

I met Leticia in Crete, the Greek Islands, where I was giving a two-week workshop. She had lost her son just eight months before, and had read many books and visited lots of Web sites, searching, seeking out anything she could on the possibility of life after death. Anything at all to help the pain, to ease the suffering, and to somehow find her son again.

In the dark, not really knowing where to go or how to find what she was looking for, not knowing what it was she really needed, her emotions drove her forward, propelled her in a desperate way to find some answers to the zillions of questions that were continually invading her mind.

Finally, she found my Web site and ordered all my books, which she read immediately. Then, her reasoning powers and common sense completely gone, with great passion and determination, she sought me out.

Not questioning her actions, not planning, not evaluating or compromising, and without a moment's hesitation, she booked the trip. Whatever happened next . . . well, that would remain to be seen.

If you haven't guessed it already, Leticia is a Fire sign, as is her son Luis. Both Bright Stars, so much the same, both thinking in the same way, both driven by the power of their elemental source of energy. Leticia was passionately seeking a way to find her son, and her son was also passionately seeking a way to find his mother, or at least a way to let her know that he was still alive. They both found me.

During the course of the next two weeks, I spoke with many parents who had lost their children, and messages of love and hope were free-flowing and amazing. Souls were reunited, including Leticia and her son—no endings, only many, many new beginnings.

With Leticia, as with some others on that trip, I formed a special bond, a friendship that was to continue and develop further. We had spoken and e-mailed two or three times since the trip, but on November 18, in the morning, Leticia called me in deep distress. "It's his birthday," she sobbed, "and I don't think I can bear it. I don't know what to do."

Luis was immediately by my side, and I began listening to him before his mother had finished speaking. He told me about the small dinner party Leticia was giving for their close family and one or two good friends. "Tell her I'll be there tonight. I want a chocolate birthday cake and candles."

"But how will I know?" sobbed his mother. "How will I be sure that he's with us?"

I calmed her down as best I could, all the while looking to her son for his help.

"Tell her I am going to blow out the candles," he said, and when I hesitated to give the message, not wanting to give false hope, I saw his true Firesign nature, the passion in his eyes, as he nodded his confirmation to my silent question. "I'll be there," he repeated firmly, "and I will blow out the candles."

Leticia's guests arrived at four in the afternoon, and she told her sons and her friends of Luis's promise. It was hard to believe. Would he really come?

The chocolate birthday cake was filled with candles. The table was perfectly set, with eighteen candles as a centerpiece, but no one paid much attention to them. It was the cake they were watching.

Struggling with her emotions, trying hard to deal with the day, with her fear of being disappointed, but trusting me and believing in her son, Leticia waited. They all waited.

It began at seven o'clock, when the candles on the table began their dance. There were no windows open, no drafts, no possible way for it to happen, and yet it did. On some candles, the flame went one way, and on some another. A few were blown out. Some flames became three flames, some grew taller, some small. Then a light in the dining room began to flicker on and off, and then the candles on the table began to dance even more beautifully.

Leticia felt him there. Her other two sons felt him there, and so did their friends. Luis had managed a manifestation of his energy. He had kept his promise, and had blown out his candles.

When I got her phone call inviting me to Miami for Christmas, I declined. It was impossible, I said. I had a book to finish.

"Well, finish it here. If you can't come for Christmas, what about January?"

I'm not sure what made me agree. Remember, I'm an Earth sign, I like to plan, to strategize, to think things through. I am not as impulsive as a Fire sign, but in that moment and without a second's hesitation, I found myself saying yes.

It was in Miami that I met Veri and Alejo, Leticia's other two sons. Veri is a Water sign, a Peacemaker Soul, and Alejo is an Earth sign, a Visionary Soul. I was able to see, firsthand, how each one's driving energy force influenced the way they dealt with their loss. Each one, through their unique energy flow, had a different approach.

For Leticia it was, it is, incredibly difficult, for her emotions often overcome her reason and she tries to hide herself away so that others won't see the torment that she's in, the feelings she does not know how to control. But Luis, her Fire-sign son, understanding her needs and reactions completely because they are the same as his own, coming from that same elemental energy force, was passionately and impatiently determined to find a way to bring help and understanding to his family.

I had fully expected that at some point during my visit to Miami I would be speaking to Luis again, but time was getting short, and although I had spoken with Luis to his brother, Alejo, I had not yet heard any messages from him to his mother. And she, surprisingly, had not asked. Respectful of my time, my energy, my need to work on the book, Leticia, acting completely out of character for a Fire sign, had decided to wait and see.

It was our last day together, and we were sitting out in the sun, just relaxing and hanging out, when I felt the tap, tap, tap on my shoulder. I didn't have to turn around to see who it was. His energy was enough—I felt it charge through me in a gentle and loving flow of emotion.

Leticia was oblivious to any change and chatted on, unnoticing of my slight shift of mood, as I began to listen, to move into the realm of the spirit world, to hear what I could, to see, to sense, and to feel what it was that the handsome young man standing beside me wanted to communicate to his mother.

As I went with him, freely giving myself up to the connection, Luis took me to the place that was most important to him right then.

"The mountain, the mountain," he repeated over and over again, "tell her she can see me on the mountain."

I turned to Leticia and asked, "Do you live near a mountain?"

Surprised by my question, and not yet understanding that Luis was with us, she nodded, telling me that she could see the mountain from her bedroom window, not in Miami but at her home in Mexico.

And so began the messages from Luis to his mother, as she hurriedly grabbed her tape recorder. He told her many things that day, and spoke lovingly of his brothers and how he would try to take care of them all. He talked of death as a beginning of a new way of life, a way of life which still included his family and his friends. He talked of ways that his mother could reach him and know that he was with her. "Watch for me on the mountain," he said, and I was reminded of the great story of Black Elk, in the book by the same name. "Watch for me on the mountain," Luis said, again and again, "and if you open your eyes and your heart, you will see me there. I will be standing on the top of the world. Tell my brothers, I will be standing on the mountain, standing on the top of the world."

The day after Leticia left Miami to go home to Mexico, she called to tell me that her son, Alejo, had heard the tape, and had heard his brother's message.

"I didn't know," Leticia told me, "but Alejo goes mountain biking with his friends on the mountain. They go and stand on the very top, and Alejo always says the same thing: 'Look, look . . . I'm standing on top of the world.'"

Knowing that we are a cluster of souls, a mix of thirteen soul signs, living and experiencing a short amount of our lives on a planet we call Earth, which is no more than a grain of sand, a speck of dust in the greater universe; knowing and coming to understand this new science and its importance to us in understanding how to make the very best of that experience is thrilling, exciting, and of continual fascination to me. There is no end to what we can learn, and the information contained in this book is only a small part of a much greater knowledge of soul signs and what it means to us.

We are souls, created from our five individual pockets of energy, coming from the universe, born of a power that is so complex and yet in some ways so simple as to baffle us, to confuse and to amaze us, both at the same time.

We are spiritual beings, part of the human soul cluster, yes, but we are also part of the power of the Holy Spirit, the God force, which embraces and protects us. And no matter what our experiences are at any given moment in time, in our relationships with others or with ourselves, and no matter what form our soul takes while we are here, human or otherwise, we should be comforted, for even though it may seem not to be, everything is a part of God's plan. The instinctive logic behind soul signs provides reassurance of that fact.

It doesn't matter that you believe one hundred percent that there is a life after death. When you lose someone you love, you need reassurance that they're okay. When we are given signs or messages from the spirit world, we are reassured. We need reassurance that we are loved, that we are cared for, that our loved ones are loved and cared for; we need reassurance that we are not alone. That we are, indeed, part of a much greater plan.

Soul signs give us that reassurance. They help us understand the differences between us all. They help us understand who we are. They help us love ourselves more. And they help us connect with each other more.

One Little Creature, Great and Small

I look back on all I have written here, knowing that it is just a small portion of what I know, and it would be hard for me to pick a favorite chapter, a part which fascinates or moves me more than another, but one group, perhaps my favorite, and one very close to my heart, is the subject of animal soul signs, and I hope in the future to write more about that.

And so this is the way I have chosen to begin the end and the beginning of the next phase of my life, with tales of hope for us all, even for those who have suffered unbearable losses. Some of you may think that there are far more moving, insightful, and more important things to tell, and you may be right—but not today, not right at this moment, for you see, even as I write, a manifestation is taking place.

You know about my Rosie, my beautiful little Brittany spaniel, from the chapter "All Creatures Great and Small."

She came to me when she was eighteen months old, and she had been harshly and cruelly treated. Consequently, when I first got her, she was very nervous and did not trust people, although she took to me immediately. She was very needy, requiring a lot of patience and gentle handling. However, she is a fighter, she has a strength, a great strength of character, and an independent spirit. She will never be cowed by anyone or anything. Definitely an Earth sign. Definitely a Warrior. A true Warrior Soul.

I found the tumor on her right foot last January, and she had surgery to remove it. Everything was fine until May, when the tumor reappeared, but this time it was much worse. As I explained earlier, she had to have her leg and shoulder removed. Her recovery was quick, so quick that it surprised even the surgeon, and I was grateful for the many healing prayers from everyone who knew, knowing that those prayers had helped to help my puppy.

Summer and fall were the best. She went swimming and frogging, she began playing with my Labrador, Niño, again, and even though she was now ten years old, I could see the puppy in her as she regained her strength. I could see the Warrior. She would not and could not be held back.

It was early December when I knew the cancer was back. One of the drawbacks of my gift—knowing when you don't want to know. I knew this was serious.

She was lying opposite me on the sofa as I was writing. She was quiet and content and not in any distress at all. Still, I knew.

Over the next weeks I tried to tell myself I was mistaken. There were no outward signs, she was eating well, playing, enjoying the outdoors, even though now it was winter and very, very cold. I had no reason to know, I had no way to know, I did not want to know. . . . And yet I knew.

Watching carefully for any sign that I was right and seeing none, I convinced myself that I was wrong. I tried to turn my back on the pain I knew was coming.

My darling Rosie passed on December 31, New Year's Eve. It was quick, and painless, and very easy for her; not so easy for me, though, or for the others who loved her.

A few weeks have passed since she has been gone, and yet I know she has not gone at all. She lies at my feet as I write, and I can feel her nose nudging my ankle. If it weren't for the pad on my lap, I know she would be up on the sofa with me, cuddling like we always do.

She is whole again, looking just as she did before the surgery. Her breath is warm on my foot, her energy vibrant and as powerful as it always was.

Reassured, having known that she would be okay but nevertheless reassured, my concerns for her well-being disappear as I look down at her and see that all is well.

"I am a Warrior Soul, Rosie," I whisper, as I struggle on the battlefield of my emotions, trying to write as I look down at her, struggling, as all Warrior signs will do, to put my emotions to one side so that I can more powerfully embrace the moment, as reassurance floods through me. It is just what I need.

She stretches her head out in front of my feet and looks up at me with those wonderful hazel eyes of hers, giving me strength and inspiration . . . one little Warrior Soul to another.

Now I feel Grey Eagle draw close, I see him standing by my side again, another Warrior Soul. I hear his voice, strong and clear, and clearly I hear him say . . .

"There is only the end of one beginning, which leads us to the beginning of another ending and another beginning. There is no final chapter . . . only life continuing on," he says. "Only life, after life . . . continuing on."

I look down at my Rosie, still lying at my feet as I have been writing, and I look back at myself, a true Warrior Soul, as indeed she is. I am comforted and greatly blessed by the knowledge of this beautiful garden of ours, our garden of souls, incredible daffodils. Each of us a separate and beautiful soul in a world of creatures great and small.

My Rosie looks back up at me. Our eyes meet, and I know it to be true. There is no final chapter.

INDEX

Underscored references indicate boxed text.

Altea, Rosemary, 4–7, 305
abuse of, as child, 37
encounter with a Dark Soul,
157–59
family dynamics of, 236–41
as gardener of souls, 81–87
Grey Eagle as teacher of, 4–5
love relationships of, 170, 233–36
as medium, 5–6
pets, 244–53, 285–88
stories of afterlife
Llewella's death, 264–75
Luis on top of the world, 279–84
Ryan's cactus, 276–79
as Warrior Soul, 5, 16
Angels
in heaven, 264
as soul guides, 34
Anger, Sulphur energy group and, 53
Animals, soul signs and, 21, 243–53
Astral travel, 23
Astrology, 12–13
Attitude change, toward others, 15–16

B

Balance
Central energy flow and, 173, 186
in relationships, 180–81
Behavior
choice and, 62–63
knowing right from wrong, 36–37
learned
effect of, on each energy group,
60
doomed relationships and, 223–27,
229

evil acts and, 151–52
in our growth process, 36–37
self-sabotage and, 224–25, 229
Birth, soul choice prior to, 34–35
Bright Star Souls
compatibility of energy, with
Newborn Souls, <u>185</u>, 188, 201
Prophet Souls, <u>185</u>, 201
dangers for, 100
description of
character traits, 99–100
general qualities, 98–99
potential negative aspects, 162
in relationships, 100
Extrovert energy flow and, 131–32
ideal mates for, <u>185</u>
incompatibility of energy, with
Hunter Souls, 188, 189
Retrospective Souls, 187, 188
Seeker Souls, 194
Traveler Souls, 177–78
Visionary Souls, 190
questions to determine, 140
in relationships, with
Dreaming Souls, 201, 208
Hunter Souls, 188
Newborn Souls, 188, 201, 202
Old Souls, 201, 204
other Bright Star Souls, 216–17
Peacemaker Souls, 201, 212
Prophet Souls, 201, 211
Retrospective Souls, 188
Visionary Souls, 201
Warrior Souls, 201, 202
Short-cupped daffodil and, 100
Bulbocodium daffodil, 117

D

P

Passivity
    characteristic of
        Air energy group, 52, 59
        Water energy group, 59
    uncharacteristic of
        Earth energy group, 59
        Fire energy group, 59
Past
    effect of, on current behavior,
        230–33
    as energy we hold on to, 227, 256
    learning from, 257
Peacemaker Souls
    balance as quality of, 173
    Central energy flow and, 135, 173
    compatibility of energy, with
        all Earth signs, 195
        Hunter Souls, <u>185</u>
        Visionary Souls, <u>185</u>, 212
        Warrior Souls, <u>185</u>, 195, 212
    dangers for, 119
    description of
        character traits of, 118–19
        general qualities of, 117–18
        potential negative aspects of, 164
        in relationships, 119
    ideal mates for, <u>185</u>
    incompatibility of energy, with
        Retrospective Souls, 195
    Jonquilla daffodil and, 119
    questions to determine, 143
    in relationships, with
        all Earth signs, 195
        Bright Star Souls, 201, 212

        Dreaming Souls, 209, 212
        Hunter Souls, 205, 212
        Newborn Souls, 203, 212
        Old Souls, 177, 203, 213
        other Peacemaker Souls, 220–21
        Prophet Souls, 211, 212
        Retrospective Souls, 195, 204, 212
        Seeker Souls, 207, 213
        Traveler Souls, 206, 213
        Visionary Souls, 212
        Warrior Souls, 195, 202, 212
People
    acceptance of differences in, 9–10
    examples of evil, 150–51
    as pure energy, 11
    wanting to change others, 10–11
Perfection, Retrospective Soul and, 94
Personality, energy type and, 12
Pets
    cats, 249–50
    dogs, 245–48, 285–88
    energy groups and, 244–45
    horses, 250–53
    Rosemary's dogs, 245–47, 285–88
    soul signs and, 253, 285–88
    Sulphur energy and, 253
Planning
    Air energy group and, 58
    Earth energy group and, 44, 51–52
    Water energy group and, 58
Playmates
    compatibility of energy, 200
    as type of soul mate, 171–72
Pockets of energy. *See* Energy groups
Poeticus daffodil, 98

ABOUT THE AUTHOR

Rosemary Altea, whose work as a medium and healer has been featured in *Vanity Fair*, *People*, and the *New York Times*, is founder of the nonprofit Rosemary Altea Association of Healers, based in England and Vermont. The best-selling author of *The Eagle and the Rose*, *Proud Spirit*, and *You Own the Power*, she is also the author of the book/audio package *Give the Gift of Healing*. She lives in Vermont.

For more information on Rosemary's books and on her audio and meditation tapes and CDs, visit her Web site at www.rosemaryaltea.com.